T0384515

RELATIONAL HEALTH

We tend to credit the healthy for good habits and discipline, and assign blame to the sick. All too often we view our health as a product of individual inputs rather than through a lens of interconnected, relational health. The relational health perspective offers an alternative way to view how our health is shaped and what the most productive avenues are for achieving long-term positive outcomes. This book draws on empirical research that illuminates how social relationships affect health outcomes, with a focus on three specific health problems: obesity, opioid use disorder, and depression in older adults. It incorporates examples of the untapped potential of community resources, social networks, and varied partnerships. The research presented is supplemented by perspectives from health care providers, patients and their families, and health policy experts, examining the role of relationships in health production and maintenance.

LAURA S. RICHMAN is a health psychologist who has published widely in the field of social drivers of health. She has been a professor at Duke University, North Carolina since 2003 and is currently a visiting professor at George Washington University. This book was developed when Richman was a fellow at the Center for Advanced Study in Behavioral Sciences at Stanford University from 2019 to 2020.

RELATIONAL HEALTH

How Social Connection Impacts Our Physical and Mental Wellbeing

LAURA S. RICHMAN

Duke University, North Carolina

Shaftesbury Road, Cambridge CB2 8EA, United Kingdom

One Liberty Plaza, 20th Floor, New York, NY 10006, USA

477 Williamstown Road, Port Melbourne, VIC 3207, Australia

314–321, 3rd Floor, Plot 3, Splendor Forum, Jasola District Centre,
New Delhi – 110025, India

103 Penang Road, #05–06/07, Visioncrest Commercial, Singapore 238467

Cambridge University Press is part of Cambridge University Press & Assessment,
a department of the University of Cambridge.

We share the University's mission to contribute to society through the pursuit of
education, learning and research at the highest international levels of excellence.

www.cambridge.org
Information on this title: www.cambridge.org/9781316515570
DOI: 10.1017/9781009025997

© Laura S. Richman 2023

First published 2023

A catalogue record for this publication is available from the British Library.

ISBN 978-1-316-51557-0 Hardback

Cambridge University Press & Assessment has no responsibility for the persistence or accuracy of
URLs for external or third-party internet websites referred to in this publication
and does not guarantee that any content on such websites is, or will remain,
accurate or appropriate.

Contents

v

Figures

Boxes

Case Studies

Acknowledgments

I began this book when I was a fellow at the Center for Advanced Study of Behavioral Sciences. I am grateful for the time and intellectual space that CASBS provided and the opportunity to get input from many wonderful fellows and affiliates during the 2019–2020 year. A special thanks to Anita Hardon, whose feedback, even after COVID forced our lovely Stanford Dish "walk-talks" to Zoom calls, was invaluable.

I have been fortunate to have worked with outstanding students over the years, who contributed to the advancement of the health inequalities work described in many of the chapters. I thank the many people who took the time to be interviewed for this book to provide details on their lived experiences or to lend their expertise. Many thanks to Cambridge University Press for their enthusiasm for this work, especially Stephen Acerra, and the generous editing provided by Michele Marietta. I am indebted to many friends, family, and colleagues who talked through ideas with me, read drafts of chapters, or otherwise provided encouragement. I was particularly fortunate that my lifelong friend Jane Kim was enthusiastically willing to provide her keen medical insights to this work.

And most importantly, I thank my family, Barak, Ariella, Eden, and Izak, for their love and wisdom.

CHAPTER I

Introduction

Key Points

- Many of the health problems we face today are widely viewed as individual problems of willpower and personal responsibility that should be dealt with through individual solutions.
- Relational health offers an alternative framework that draws on the role of relationships for prevention and treatment efforts to improve health outcomes.
- Obesity, opioid use disorder, and depression in older adults are presented as case studies to illustrate the applicability of a relational health framework for integrating relational contexts and aspects of the health care system.

Introduction to Relational Health

Even with all the extraordinary twentieth-century advances in medicine, good health is elusive to far too many in the United States. Despite health care spending that far exceeds that of other wealthy countries, technological innovations, and unprecedented knowledge about risk factors for disease, we are struggling with unacceptably high rates of chronic illness. Research from a range of disciplines including epidemiology, psychology, sociology, behavioral medicine, and population health show that the web of social relationships that surround us have significant effects on our behaviors and outcomes. An approach to health that considers these realities aligns better with how we live our lives and what we need to thrive.

The goal of this book is to provide an overview of what *relational health* means in the context of where we live, work, and play, and how it can be applied as a framework for achieving better health and wellbeing. Instead of considering populations as a collection of individuals, the premise of relational health suggests that populations instead should be considered as individuals who are interconnected with each other. Our relationships, including family, friends, and acquaintances, can all provide valuable information (which doctor to see, where local club sports are offered, how to find childcare), essential social support (transportation to medical appointments, loans to cushion the costs of health care, a cheerleader for health goals), and positive social norms (role modeling self-care). Of course, social relationships are not all good – many can be negative by providing bad information, encouraging bad health habits, or creating collective injury from violence. These influences, *both good and bad,* are essential to our understanding of how best to promote health and how to improve how care is provided.

Medical practitioners and policymakers largely do not emphasize these factors as avenues to better health, despite the deep evidence base for the important role that relationship factors play in influencing behaviors and outcomes. For a host of reasons that will be addressed in this chapter, our health care system is organized to treat patients as individuals, devoid of context. Relational health suggests that there are missed opportunities in viewing illness through only an individual lens. It offers a framework for considering how an individual's networks of relationships can promote or undermine healthy behavior. Understanding the influence of relationships can lead to prevention and treatment efforts that are more consistent with how people live their lives.

This book focuses on three health challenges: obesity, opioid use disorder, and depression in older adults, all of which increase vulnerability to other diseases and premature mortality. These health issues are particularly poignant examples of the lost opportunities to reduce suffering and improve outcomes when the individualized approach continues to predominate prevention and treatment efforts. For decades, a wide variety of (nonrelational) medical interventions have been deployed to address these health issues, with disappointing progress. Although the research and examples provided in these chapters are centered around obesity, opioid use disorder, and depression, the list of chronic health conditions that we grapple with and suffer from continues to grow at an alarming rate, and the relational health framework can and should be applied more broadly.

Relationships as Essential Drivers of Health

A fundamental concept worth emphasizing at the outset is that our health is multiply determined. Accordingly, relationships are an important and underestimated contributor, but also need to be understood as one of many contributors that influence our health over the course of our lives. Other nonmedical drivers of health, often referred to as "social determinants of health," include factors such as safe housing, transportation, and socioeconomic conditions such as income, wealth, and education. Despite the often complicated ways in which social factors affect health – some operate through indirect behavioral pathways, others function through more direct biological mechanisms; some have short-term effects, whereas others show their effects over the course of a lifetime; and for some it is not entirely clear how they impact health and for whom – public health and medical provider thought leaders, Drs. Paula Braverman and Laura Gottlieb have argued, it is past time to take seriously these contributions. They have noted, "The consistency and reproducibility of strong associations between social factors and a multitude of health outcomes in diverse settings and populations have been well-documented, and the biological plausibility of the influence of social factors on health has been established."[1] The relational health approach does not claim that relationships are the only avenue to improve health outcomes, but rather that they are a crucially important social determinant for which we have strong evidence and robust strategies to improve health beyond the entrenched individualized approaches. They are important enough to be a central component both in treating individuals and in promoting widespread population health.

To best understand the pathways through which relationships influence health, a multilevel perspective is a framework that situates relationships in a broader sociocultural context. Social networks have been defined as the web of social relationships that surround an individual and the characteristics of those ties. A conceptual model for how social networks impact health was created by Berkman and colleagues (Figure 1.1). Their model emphasizes dynamically linked processes beginning with the macro-social context or "upstream factors." The assumption of this model is that social networks are contained within larger social and cultural contexts which shape and sustain the structure of networks. These macro factors help us to understand that the relationships in which we are embedded are determined by the context and culture in which we live, which include socioeconomic factors, politics, and social change.

[1] Braveman, P., & Gottlieb, L. (2014). The social determinants of health: it's time to consider the causes of the causes. *Public Health Reports* 129(Suppl. 2): 19–31. https://doi.org/10.1177/00333549141291S206

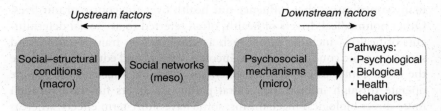

Figure 1.1 Conceptual model of how social networks impact health. Modified from Berkman et al.[2]

The model's downstream factors are the influences that network structure and function have on behavior and ultimately health, including the pathways of provision of social support, social influence, social engagement and attachment, and access to resources and material goods. Importantly, not all of these network influences are positive, and there is variation in the type, frequency, intensity, and extent of support provided. In this book the focus is largely on the downstream psychosocial mechanisms by which social networks impact health, but the upstream, social structural conditions that shape social networks need to be integrated into our understanding of how interventions are designed and policy is constructed. Socioeconomic factors, for example, will necessarily shape the extent to which people can benefit from social support opportunities and social influences vary by demographics.

Despite the broad health implications of relationship factors and the social contexts in which they are embedded, these influences tend to be underestimated. In a stark example of this, psychology researchers collected crowd-sourced data in the United States and United Kingdom and found that members of the public dramatically misjudge the importance of social factors for health and mortality.[3] The study participants, the majority of whom had a college education, exhibited a strong capacity to estimate the relative importance of certain behavioral risk factors, such as smoking. However, the study participants were extremely poor at estimating the impact of relationship factors such as social support and social integration and other social factors. The researchers considered whether demographic characteristics of the participants, such as age, gender, nationality, and level of contact

[2] Berkman, L. F., Glass, T., Brissette, I., & Seeman, T. E. (2000). From social integration to health: Durkheim in the new millennium. *Social Science & Medicine* 51(6): 843–857. https://doi.org/10.1016/s0277-9536(00)00065-4

[3] Haslam, S. A., McMahon, C., Cruwys, T., et al. (2018). Social cure, what social cure? The propensity to underestimate the importance of social factors for health. *Social Science & Medicine* 198: 14–21. https://doi.org/10.1016/j.socscimed.2017.12.020

with the medical profession, could potentially explain the results. Although their results were explained in part by sex, age, education, and ideological factors – with men, younger participants, those with lower education, and more conservative ideology all being more likely to underestimate the importance of relationship and other social factors, the effects still remained even after including these variables in the analyses. The authors concluded that, "In the Western world at least, the idea that family, friends, work colleagues, and social groups more generally have a key role to play in helping us overcome a range of stressors – including illness, traumatic life-changes, and discriminatory treatment – does not appear to be all that intuitive."[4]

My expertise on relational health developed from many years of studying how people's health is affected by social devaluation. When people have identities that are devalued, such as racial minorities, women in male-dominated professions, and people with low socioeconomic status, they experience an unwelcome lack of social connection in many contexts of their lives. What my students, colleagues, and I found in our research studies is that experiences of devaluation, such as stigmatization, discrimination, and rejection, contribute to health inequalities for disadvantaged groups.

These social stigmas impose negative mental and physical health consequences.[5] Rejection, discrimination, and stigmatization can take a psychological toll, elevating our risk for anxiety and depression. Our bodies respond to social devaluation physically as well. Research from our lab and numerous others has found that in response to a social threat such as discrimination, the body reacts as if we are under threat by releasing stress hormones, elevating the heart rate, and subjective experiences of stress.[6] One explanation for why we respond this way is because these experiences of devaluation threaten our evolutionary drive to function within social groups and depend on other people for survival. This

---

[4] Jetten, J., Haslam, C., & Haslam, S. A. (Eds.) (2012). *The Social Cure: Identity, Health and Well-being*. Psychology Press.

[5] Pascoe, E., & Richman, L. S. (2009). Perceived discrimination and health: a meta-analytic review. *Psychological Bulletin* 135: 531–554.

[6] Richman, L. S., Bennett, G., Pek, J., Siegler, I. C., & Williams, R. B. (2007). Discrimination, dispositions, and cardiovascular responses to stress. *Health Psychology* 26: 675–683; Richman, L. S., & Jonassaint, C. (2008). The effects of race-related stress on cortisol reactivity in the laboratory: implications of the Duke Lacrosse scandal. *Annals of Behavioral Medicine* 35: 105–110; Richman, L. S., Pek, J., Pascoe, E., & Bauer, D. (2010). The effects of perceived discrimination on ambulatory blood pressure and affective responses to interpersonal stress modeled over 24 hours. *Health Psychology* 29: 403–411.

repeated over-activation of physiological systems in a stress state is ultimately one indirect pathway through which social devaluation can then increase vulnerability to certain illnesses.

My collaborators and I have also found that these particular kinds of experiences of social devaluation can lead to risky health behaviors, such as substance use and overindulging in high-caloric foods. For example, in one experiment we found that when research participants received performance feedback from a biased evaluator and immediately afterwards were offered the choice between a healthy granola bar or a high-caloric candy bar, they more often choose the candy option as compared to a neutral feedback control group.[7] In other research, we found similar results with an increased tendency to engage in unhealthy substance use in response to discrimination.[8] People may be inclined to turn to less healthy choices and behaviors in response to discrimination because they can provide comfort, are familiar, and may at least temporarily alleviate stress. Discrimination is also associated with the inhibition of health-promoting behaviors, such as exercise and other preventive care.[9]

Our research has implications for the design of relational solutions for health issues that carry the weight of stigmatization, as is the case for the examples that are the focus of this book. Despite increased public understanding and public health campaigns to reduce stigma, obesity, substance use, and mental health disorders are still socially devalued. Evidence suggests that stigmatizing and shaming people toward behavior change (a strategy that is based on an individualized approach to health) is ineffective and harmful. Numerous studies show that perceived stigmatization and discrimination are associated with higher levels of unhealthy behavior, not positive behavior change. And yet this strategy is still frequently employed.

Support seeking from family, friends, neighbors, or health care providers is also more difficult when people feel devalued by their health status. Indeed, becoming socially isolated and refusing support are

---

[7] Pascoe, E. A., & Richman, L. S. (2011). Effects of discrimination on food decisions. *Self & Identity* 10: 396–406.

[8] Richman, L. S., Boynton, M. H., Costanzo, P., & Banas, K. (2013). Interactive effects of discrimination and racial identity on alcohol-related thoughts and use. *Basic and Applied Social Psychology* 35: 396–407; Stock, M., Gibbons, F., Beekman, J., Williams, K., Richman, L. S., & Gerrard, M. (2018). Racial (vs. self) affirmation as a protective mechanism against the effects of racial exclusion on negative affect and substance use vulnerability among black young adults. *Journal of Behavioral Medicine* 41: 195–207; Boynton, M., & Richman, L. S. (2014). An online daily diary study of alcohol use using Amazon's Mechanical Turk. *Drug and Alcohol Review* 33: 456–461.

[9] Lattanner, M., Pascoe, E., & Richman, L. S. (2022). Meta-analysis of interpersonal discrimination and health-related behaviors. *Health Psychology* 41(5), 319–331.

hallmarks of opioid use disorder, which is highly stigmatized. Although the need for social connection is strong, the limited capacity to seek out and sustain support opportunities may play a critical role in determining how members of stigmatized groups may be vulnerable to negative long-term effects on health and wellbeing. Maintaining healthy, supportive relationships can be difficult for many, particularly those who have experienced stigma, and it is crucial to build on strong examples of communities of care and services that already exist in order to connect with people who may be difficult to reach.

Recent health trends make it clear that new strategies for dealing with these health challenges are greatly needed. The current methods of treating the individual do not work in the ways we are led to believe they should. Obesity rates, for example, are predicted to only increase over time. In 2019, Harvard researchers published a study forecasting that by 2030 nearly one-half of adults will be obese and nearly one-quarter of adults will be severely obese.[10] Those who are obese have higher risks of illnesses that can compromise quality of life, such as diabetes, heart disease, and several types of cancer.

An emphasis on the individual responsibility to maintain a healthy diet and weight is not a useful mindset for most people. When repeated attempts to lose weight fall short, people often feel worthless or desperate. These feelings can lead to expensive, trendy, or sham approaches to weight loss that are not shown to be effective over time.[11] More promising programs are those that use a less individualized, "go-it-alone" approach and instead incorporate supportive, nonstigmatizing, and community-based strategies to healthy eating and weight management. Weight loss programs that rely on support mechanisms rather than encouraging weight loss through sheer willpower increase weight management effectiveness. For example, when participants in a commercial weight loss program chose a weight loss "buddy," they lost more weight and waist inches after 15 weeks of participation than those who participated in the program without buddy support.[12] The buddy system has also shown success when it comes to sticking to an exercise program.

[10] Ward, Z. J., Bleich, S., Cradock, A., et al. (2019). Projected U.S. state-level prevalence of adult obesity and severe obesity. *NEJM* 381(25): 2440–2450.

[11] Puhl, R. M., & Heuer, C. A. (2010). Obesity stigma: important considerations for public health. *American Journal of Public Health* 100(6): 1019–1028.

[12] Dailey, R., Romo, L., Myer, S., et al. (2018). The buddy benefit: increasing the effectiveness of an employee-targeted weight-loss program. *Journal of Health Communication* 23(3): 272–280. https://doi.org/10.1080/10810730.2018.1436622

As with obesity, chronic pain (the most common root cause of opioid use disorder, including both physical and psychological pain) has long been treated as an individualized problem to solve within the health care system and, also like obesity, the individualized approach has had disappointing progress in improving people's lives.

Case Study 1.1: Jen[13]

Jen is a single, middle-aged accountant who for over two years experienced disabling lower back pain. Her experiences trying to find relief from her pain are frustratingly common. Neither her primary care physician nor three orthopedic and neurosurgical consultants were able to determine what was causing the pain. The imaging examinations revealed no significant pathology, nor did other tests. She was placed in the amorphous medical category of "unexplained symptoms/chronic pain." Over time she developed a tense relationship with her primary care doctor over her requests for opioid pain relief.

Jen's continued pain led her to seek care at the University of Washington's multidisciplinary pain clinic, where she had the good fortune to be seen by Dr. Kleinman, a psychiatrist and cultural anthropologist. In his book *The Soul of Care*, he describes how, after hearing her history, it was apparent to him that Jen had all the symptoms of depressive disorder with the added hazard of addiction to medications. After drawing her out, he understood that obesity and depression contributed to her chronic pain in ways that had never been explored by all the specialists she consulted. Even more, Dr. Kleinman was able to see that the physical pain was a symptom of larger issues for which the source and solutions involved her social relationships. In his practice, he emphasizes that focusing only on someone's pain, and considering that pain only from a disease perspective, misses the context of the life of the sufferer.

Many patients are like Jen. A 2018 CDC report indicates that approximately 50 million people in the United States suffer from chronic pain that is not responsive to medical treatment.[14] This lack of improvement can be very frustrating for physicians who recognize that many patients who present for pain are also grappling with a host of other factors that contribute to the pain. However, the opportunity to understand the context of pain is typically lost in a clinical encounter, as is the opportunity

---

[13] Kleinman, A. (2019). *The Soul of Care: The Moral Education of a Husband and a Doctor*. Penguin.
[14] Dahlhamer, J. (2018). Prevalence of chronic pain and high-impact chronic pain among adults: United States, 2016. *MMWR: Morbidity and Mortality Weekly Report*, 67. https://doi.org/10.15585/mmwr.mm6736a2.

to understand the relations that amplify the pain and to develop construct-ive solutions to reduce its impact.

For older adults, depressive symptoms are frequently viewed as a normal part of aging, and this erroneous belief in the inevitability of depression in old age can hinder opportunities for prevention and treatment. Depression is more accurately characterized as a complex product of biological, psy-chological, and social factors. Social isolation and loneliness in older adults have been shown to be significant risk factors for depressive symptoms, and depression can also lead to social isolation.

The Status Quo: Structural Causes

There are many reasons why the relational health perspective has not gotten more traction in how health care is delivered. Consider why the US health care system is organized around an individualized approach to understanding and treating patients. How we pay for health care – a complex issue that is not the focus of this book, but is clearly relevant to the persistence of the current model and a barrier to uptake of a relational approach – structurally supports the individualized model. Health care providers are compensated for services they provide; they get paid for diagnosing and treating individual patients with conspicuous medical care. Thus, there is little incentive for health care professionals to identify underlying causes of disease and disorders. The most recent International Classification of Diseases, Tenth Revision (ICD-10), which defines the codes that providers enter in their patients' electronic health records, includes codes specifically for psychosocial risk and economic determinant-related codes, called "Z codes." Despite the increasing use of a Z code that enables health care providers to document social needs – for example, one of the top five Z codes utilized in 2019 among fee-for-service Medicare beneficiaries was "Problems related to living alone" – providers are not able to bill for these social needs and so, most often, they are left unaddressed.[15]

The United States is home to many deeply compassionate physicians and other health care providers who want to help their patients as much as possible. However, many of them report that there are limitations on their ability to understand and address the root causes of patients' suffering.

[15] Maksut, J. L., Hodge, C., Van, C. D., Razmi, A., & Khau, M. T. (2021). Utilization of Z codes for social determinants of health among Medicare fee-for-service beneficiaries, 2019. Office of Minority Health (OMH) Data Highlight No. 24. Centers for Medicare and Medicaid Services (CMS), Baltimore, MD.

Constraints on the provider–patient relationship contribute to difficulties in identifying and addressing social needs in the context of a health care visit. To understand the personal aspects of a patient's life requires a trusting relationship between the provider and patient and many factors constrain the development of such a relationship. A typical medical appointment is short (usually 15–20 minutes), which often doesn't allow for attention to social factors. Establishing a trusting relationship is also impaired by limited points of contact due to, among other factors, fractured care where a patient may see a host of different providers rather than a consistent one.

The training of physicians and many other kinds of health care providers often does not include exploring social and emotional pain and other factors that are outside of biomedical influences. Many providers feel inadequately trained to do the kind of interviewing that is required to identify a complex medical issue that is caused by or coupled with significant psychosocial aspects, and their work setting is often not equipped to help them solve it.

In many ways, the health care setting is designed to focus almost entirely on biomedical factors that can be treated as efficiently as possible. This approach may seem to be a logical way to deliver health care to those who need it most. An individual comes to the doctor's office with an ailment – not a family, a community, or a neighborhood. But, as demonstrated by the millions of people in this country who seek treatment in the health care system and fail to find relief, too much is missed with this system of delivery.

The deep-rooted American approach to dealing with health issues for each individual continues for reasons that extend far beyond traditions and constraints in the health care system. Cultural norms and cognitive biases are also important contributors.

The Status Quo: Cultural and Cognitive Causes

Self-care has become popularized as an essential set of behaviors for our mental and physical health. The *Oxford Dictionary* defines self-care as the practice of acting to preserve or improve one's own health.[16] For many, self-care means preserving time in the day to focus on what are viewed as *self* needs such as exercise, sleep, or indulgences in consumer behavior that are intended to bring pleasure. Interestingly, the World Health

---

[16] www.lexico.com/definition/self-care.

Organization (WHO), a specialized agency of the United Nations responsible for international public health, defines self-care differently. While the WHO encourages higher levels of self-efficacy, autonomy, and personal responsibility, it also emphasizes the relational components of self-care: "the ability of individuals, families and communities to promote health, prevent disease, maintain health, and to cope with illness and disability with or without the support of a healthcare provider."[17] The difference here is that the WHO definition also suggests that self-care "is a broad concept" and goes on to include nutrition, lifestyle, environmental, and socioeconomic factors, among others. However, it also includes aspects "of the greater community" as a fundamental principle of self-care.

The American ideal of the "individual" teaches us to believe that each of us are solely responsible for the behaviors that lead to our poor health outcomes. The *person* is the one who is perceived as making poor choices through overindulging in unhealthy foods, failing to follow health guidelines, and giving in to urges. As such, our health care is logically organized to treat and manage individual patients.

Mainstream US culture amplifies the message that health depends on responsible personal lifestyle choices. Cultural psychologists Cayce Hook and Hazel Markus note that although the United States is composed of a wide range of cultures – each of which can have distinctive approaches to health and wellness – broad patterns can be observed nationally in how health tends to be conceptualized, discussed, and pursued.[18] Hook and Markus emphasize that even though the causes of ill health are complex, the answers offered by mainstream US culture are extremely narrow: *poor personal choices* are the primary cause of ill health, and *more personal responsibility* is the primary solution.

Our unique American culture lends itself to an individualistic approach to achieving optimal health. We value making our own decisions about substances we consume or inhale. We also want to be equally unconstrained in our decisions about whether we exercise, visit a doctor, or follow instructions of any sort. We are constantly socialized to accept these messages of personal responsibility for health. Fast-food corporations present unhealthy options to their customers while emphasizing their support for people's "freedom" to

[17] WHO (2019). WHO consolidated guideline on self-care interventions for health: sexual and reproductive health and rights. Retrieved from: www.ncbi.nlm.nih.gov/books/NBK544155.
[18] Hook, C. J., & Rose Markus, H. (2020). Health in the United States: are appeals to choice and personal responsibility making Americans sick? *Perspectives on Psychological Science* 15(3): 643–664. https://doi.org/10.1177/1745691619896252

choose.[19] Burger King's famous "Have It Your Way" slogan was recently scrapped after forty years, in favor of the more personal "Be Your Way," which, according to Burger King, is intended to remind people that "they can and should live how they want anytime." Alcohol companies spend millions on advertisements that promote drinking but that place the responsibility on consumers to "drink responsibly."[20] Magazines tout headlines on healthy lifestyles, such as "Nearly Half of U.S. Deaths Can Be Prevented with Lifestyle Changes."[21] Public health agencies instruct that "by living a healthy lifestyle, you can help keep your blood pressure, cholesterol, and blood sugar levels normal."[22] Regardless of political affiliation, government officials endorse personal responsibility: former President Barack Obama said "We've got to have the American people doing something *about their own care*" (emphasis added), while former Vice President Mike Pence argued for "bringing freedom and individual responsibility back to American health care."[23] In media and popular culture and in public statements by government and industry, these same messages of personal responsibility for health are amplified. When the effects of recommended calorie restriction and exercise increase are either negligible or only successful in the short term, the failures are attributed to poor motivation and too brief adherence to recommended lifestyle changes.

Markus and Conner offer a model of cultural influence that is represented in Figure 1.2. It shows the interacting levels of the mainstream US culture cycle of choice and personal responsibility. All four levels are assumed to be equally important, and none are assumed to take priority over the others. The arrows from one level to another indicate that cultures are dynamic, and all levels of the culture cycle continually influence each other: a change in one level can instigate changes in others.

Cultural norms influence how behavior change programs are designed. Can we nudge an individual to improve eating or exercise habits? Can we improve an individual's access to health care? We think that the source of

[19] How fast food uses the illusion of choice to feed Americans junk. Retrieved from www.yahoo.com /now/fast-food-uses-illusion-choice-100015992.html.
[20] Smith, K. C., Cukier, S., & Jernigan, D. H. (2014). Defining strategies for promoting product through "drink responsibly" messages in magazine ads for beer, spirits and alcopops. *Drug and Alcohol Dependence* 142: 168–173. https://doi.org/10.1016/j.drugalcdep.2014.06.007
[21] Park, A. (2014). 40% of US deaths can be prevented each year: here's how. *Time*. Retrieved from https://time.com/84514/nearly-half-of-us-deaths-can-be-prevented-with-lifestyle-changes.
[22] Centers for Disease Control and Prevention: National Center for Chronic Disease Prevention and Health Promotion, Division for Heart Disease and Stroke Prevention (2020). *Prevent Heart Disease, 2020*. CDC.
[23] Khullar, D. (2018). You're sick: whose fault is that? *New York Times*. Retrieved from www .nytimes.com/2018/01/10/upshot/youre-sick-whose-fault-is-that.html.

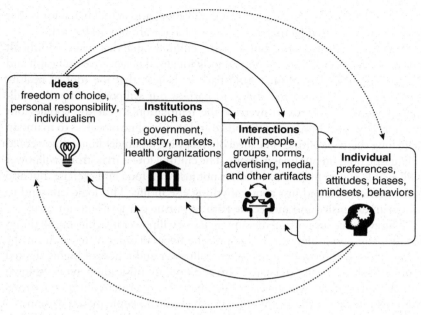

Figure 1.2 The interacting levels of the mainstream US culture cycle of choice and personal responsibility developed by Drs. Hazel Markus and Alana Conner.[24]

health comes from the individual, and so we target health problems by making individual interventions.

The problem with an overemphasis on individual factors is that these beliefs crowd out support for other factors that are more grounded in valid scientific evidence. Our day-to-day lives are filled with industry-supported temptations that are extremely hard to combat. The processed-food industry alone spends more than $4 billion a year tempting us to eat these foods that have been proven to jeopardize our health. Targeted advertising of these products to children ensures that these habits develop early, with some marketing experts finding that brand loyalty may form in children as young as two years old.[25] Everyday environments can make healthy behaviors difficult and expensive, while unhealthy behaviors are often exactly the opposite: cheap, convenient, widely promoted, and habit-forming. The

[24] Markus, H. R., & Conner, A. (2014). *Clash! How to Thrive in a Multicultural World*. Plume.
[25] Comiteau, J. (2003, March 24). When does brand loyalty start? www.adweek.com/brand-marketing/when-does-brand-loyalty-start-62841.

result of this misalignment of cultural narratives and actual behavior is that the more influential factors that shape behavior are not addressed.

Willpower is a separate – but related – cultural value that makes it difficult for policymakers to think beyond an individualized perspective on health and health care. Popular culture would have us believe that the root of healthy decision-making lies in the ability to harness our willpower. Superior willpower would enable us to override the temptation to eat the cookies our friendly coworker brought to the office and to discipline ourselves to maintain a lifelong exercise routine. The ideal of possessing an unyielding willpower has a fantastic hold on our imaginations. The cultural lore is that strong willpower will enable you to make good choices not just with food and exercise, but also with money, sex, and just about anything else in life. This logic can send us down an expensive and ineffective path to pursue our goals on our own.

The evidence supporting the supremacy of willpower in achieving all things good is disappointingly weak. Despite the hype, decades of research on the cause-and-effect relationship between willpower and a host of highly desired outcomes have been overstated. In addition to misleading or overblown conclusions, many willpower studies have been criticized for a narrow-minded perspective about the ways in which most people make decisions.

One example is the "marshmallow test," which has been canonized in American culture as a demonstration of the power and deep importance of willpower.[26] The series of experiments was devised in the late 1960s at Stanford by psychology professor Walter Mischel. The basic paradigm is that children are given a single marshmallow that they can eat right away. They are also told that if they want to, they can wait for a predetermined amount of time and if they don't eat the first marshmallow, then they will get a second marshmallow. There are adorable video recordings of children agonizing over the decision to take the prize in front of them or to delay gratification. You can see the kids turning their backs to the table with the marshmallow, coaching themselves to resist, and contorting their faces in agony over their choices (Figure 1.3).

A follow-up study on the same participants in the 1990s found astounding results: Those people who as children were able to delay gratification by resisting eating the marshmallow to hold out for the promise of two had better school performance and overall better economic success.[27] The much-touted conclusion was that the capacity to delay gratification was

[26] Mischel, W. (2015). *The Marshmallow Test.* Transworld.
[27] Shoda, Y., Mischel, W., & Peake, P. K. (1990). Predicting adolescent cognitive and self-regulatory competencies from preschool delay of gratification: identifying diagnostic conditions. *Developmental Psychology* 26(6): 978–986.

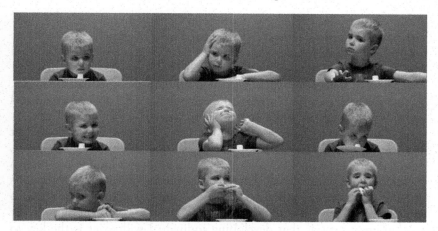

Figure 1.3 The marshmallow test.

a particularly important trait for success in life. However, follow-up studies from other researchers call these strong conclusions into question. Replication of these studies with children from varying socioeconomic backgrounds find that socioeconomic status was an overlooked explanatory variable. Higher socioeconomic status was actually a better determinant of future long-term success than whether participants held out for a second marshmallow.[28]

Moreover, growing evidence in psychology and public health finds that intense striving – what many would consider to be highly skilled will-power – can also be toxic for health. This seems to be especially the case for low-income Black men, as shown in pioneering research by social epidemiologist Sherman James in what he has coined "John Henryism."[29] Other studies have found that among African-American adolescents who come from low socioeconomic backgrounds, exhibiting high levels of self-control is associated with high academic achievement but worse physical health. In an analysis of almost 10,000 participants from the National Longitudinal Study of Adolescent to Adult Health (Add Health), Black youth from the most disadvantaged backgrounds who showed high levels of striving and perseverance in academic pursuits at age 16 were more likely to suffer from type 2 diabetes at age twenty-nine, despite exhibiting better

[28] Watts, T. W., Duncan, G. J., & Quan, H. (2018). Revisiting the marshmallow test: a conceptual replication investigating links between early delay of gratification and later outcomes. *Psychological Science* 29(7): 1159–1177. https://doi.org/10.1177/0956797618761661

[29] James, S. A. (1994). John Henryism and the health of African-Americans. *Culture, Medicine and Psychiatry* 18(2): 163–182. https://doi.org/10.1007/BF01379448

mental health and higher socioeconomic status compared to their less-striving counterparts. However, this pattern was not observed in the White subsample, where striving was associated with better mental and physical health. This phenomenon has been labeled "skin-deep resilience" to reflect the connection between striving for success (defined as graduating college, having a greater personal income, and fewer symptoms of depression) and the heightened chance of having a chronic disease.[30]

Willpower clearly helps us to set goals and follow through on them, but the scientific evidence points to a much smaller role than other factors, which do not lend themselves to easy fixes. Willpower has limited success in maintaining individual behavior change when community behaviors stay the same. Yet, the perceived benefits of superior willpower continue to guide our judgments about what matters most for good health. If the predominant view is that developing individual willpower is the key to achieving health, the result is that other types of approaches (e.g., relational approaches) can seem less relevant.

A consequence of us placing personal responsibility and willpower over everything else is that health conditions are often described in terms of individual moral failings. People who are overweight or fall into chronic substance use to manage pain and are commonly viewed either as lacking self-control or the morals necessary to make good decisions. Isolated older adults are often regarded not so much in moral terms, but more as an inevitability for which little can be done. These negative judgments reinforce arguments for individual solutions, even when structural changes are necessary. What would it look like if we saw these conditions as not merely individual moral failings, but conditions that are consequences of environmental conditions that could be mitigated with proper attention? Could acknowledging the relational dimensions of individuals bring greater health improvements than just treating the "moral failure" alone? It would mean not only improving the condition of the individual but of the people around that individual, family, and community. Strategies that consider relational health may help us do that.

Our individualized perspective on health is also a product of cognitive biases that guide how we judge behavior. Cultures (like that of the United States) that value self-determination and individualism tend to teach that we live in a fair world – one in which people are responsible for their life situations and get what they deserve. Furthermore, when we are attributing

[30] Brody, G. H., Yu, T., Miller, G. E., & Chen, E. (2016). Resilience in adolescence, health, and psychosocial outcomes. *Pediatrics* 138(6). https://doi.org/10.1542/peds.2016-1042

causes to our own behaviors, such as why we made unhealthy food choices yesterday, we are more likely to make external (circumstantial) attributions than when we are explaining the behavior of others, particularly when the behavior is undesirable. In other words, the judgments we make about ourselves and others are based on different perspectives and different information, which can lead to incorrect assumptions. For influences on eating behavior, strong evidence suggests that even though there are large variations in what and how people eat, certain universals exist across race, social class, gender, age, and geographic location. Factors that include who you eat your meals with, how much time you have for meals, and what access you have to healthy food impact *what* and *how much* you eat. In short, abundant research finds that we make less healthy food choices when we feel stress, time pressure, or have limited options.[31]

But although we can recognize these connections in our own behavior, we tend to have trouble considering how similar factors influence decision-making for others. These biases help to explain how the allowances we give for our own lapses of healthy behavior ("I was rushing to meetings all day," "I was feeling stressed") are especially difficult to see in people who have vastly different life experiences than our own. The disconnect between how we view our own behavior and how we attribute the behavior of others to internal causes (lack of willpower) encourages maintaining individual solutions, regardless of whether they work. Untrammeled individualism is the cultural status quo that hurts our individual health and the health of populations.

Although individual factors such as strength of will, grit, motivation, and related constructs all contribute to better health, what has been underestimated, and therefore missing the mark when it comes to addressing behavior change and health maintenance, is the relational basis for these personality characteristics. The evidence clearly establishes that social relationships significantly contribute to the development and maintenance of these personal strengths. More broadly, understanding the science behind relational health should force us to resist an individualized view of ourselves. We tend to credit the healthy for good habits and discipline and assign blame to the sick. All too often, and to our detriment, we view our health as a product of individual inputs rather than through a lens of interconnected, relational health.

---

[31] Mann, T. (2015). *Secrets From the Eating Lab: The Science of Weight Loss, the Myth of Willpower, and Why You Should Never Diet Again.* Harper Wave.

Relational Health in Action

The relational health perspective offers a different lens through which to view how our health is shaped and what the most productive avenues are for achieving long-term positive health outcomes. This book draws on empirical research into how social relationships affect health outcomes, with a focus on three specific health problems – obesity, opioid use disorder, and depression in older adults – and incorporates examples of the untapped potential of community resources, social networks, and varied partnerships. This research presented in the book is supplemented by perspectives from health care providers, patients and their families, and health policy experts to examine the role of relationships in health production and maintenance.

Chapter 2 describes four types of relational features: social support, social integration, social capital, and social norms, collectively referred to as the "four socials." The ways in which each of these relational factors impact health can be understood as operating through psychological, behavioral, and biological pathways. This chapter presents the definitional distinctions between the four socials and describes the scientific evidence for their pathways.

Chapter 3 focuses specifically on research findings for how obesity, opioid use disorder, and depression in older adults are impacted and shaped by the four socials. The wide range of research contexts and methods are highlighted to provide a clear understanding of the scope of work in these areas.

Chapter 4 examines the historical trends of how these three health issues have increased in prevalence over the last several decades. The chapter describes the current guidelines and practices for how health care is delivered for these patient populations and draws from perspectives and stories from health care settings.

Chapter 5 examines how a relational approach addresses avenues for prevention and sustainable solutions with a focus on four areas of emphasis. These include: improving community-level prevention efforts through building on social resources in the community through place-based strategies and communication infrastructure; reducing structural stigma in representations of health issues and individual-level stigma in provision of care; social prescribing that identifies risk and protective network characteristics in the clinical encounter and bridges primary care and community resources; and relationship building between the provider and patient and among providers. The chapter describes strategies and examples of successful programs that effectively integrate relational health themes in their treatment approaches with examples derived from interviews with patients and providers.

Chapter 6 focuses on policy priorities centered around the themes of better integration of social and medical services, improving community assets, and health care workforce improvements that include training in identifying and responding to relational needs.

Chapter 7 concludes with the broad potential for relational health to improve health and wellbeing. It considers challenges and lessons from COVID-19 and what we have learned to improve population health in the future. Priorities of prevention, mitigation, and provision of care are emphasized along with reflections on obstacles to change.

CHAPTER 2

How Social Relationships Matter for Health

Key Points

- The "four socials" – social support, social integration, social capital, social norms – have vital roles in our health, both to our benefit and detriment.
- These relational factors exert their influence through psychological, behavioral, and biological pathways.
- The harmful health effects of social disconnection illustrate the broad impact of insufficient relational ties.

Introduction

This chapter describes the broad evidence that links social relationships to health outcomes. The strongest evidence for the association between relationships and health stems from work on social support, social integration, social capital, and social norms, or "the four socials." Although there is overlap between these relationship factors and these terms are often used interchangeably, there are important distinctions between them in how they impact various behaviors and health outcomes. These distinctions, in turn, have implications for how to harness each to improve the conditions that are the focus of this book. Chapter 3 investigates how these relational factors are relevant to obesity, opioid use disorder, and depression in older adults in contributing to the production and maintenance of these conditions.

In this chapter, the descriptions of what the four socials are and how they impact health is guided by a basic model, represented in Figure 2.1, that was developed by relationships researcher Bert Uchino. As shown, the likely pathways by which relationships influence health are through our psychological, behavioral, and biological responses. The evidence and specifics of how each of the four socials exert their influence is

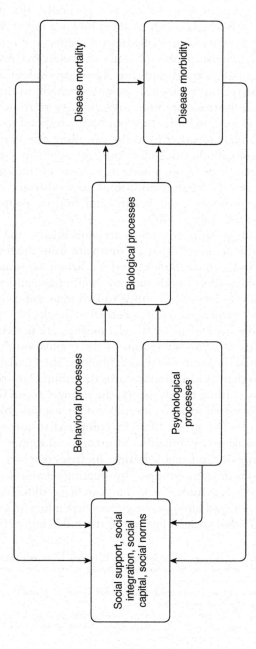

Figure 2.1 A broad model highlighting potential pathways linking social relationships and physical health. Modified from Uchino.[1]

[1] Uchino, B. N. (2006). Social support and health: a review of physiological processes potentially underlying links to disease outcomes. *Journal of Behavioral Medicine* 29(4): 377–387. https://doi.org/10.1007/s10865-006-9056-5

detailed in the sections that follow, but generally, the psychological pathway describes how relationships affect how we might make sense of our experiences, how we cope with stressful events, and our moods and emotions. Our relationships also influence our behaviors in ways that can be health-promoting or health-limiting. These psychological and behavioral responses shape our biological responses, which, in turn, affect our risk for disease and premature mortality. Positive relationship features, most notably, can serve to buffer how our bodies respond to stress. In this way, we are less likely to suffer from the cascading effects that stress can have on how our bodies regulate our metabolism, our hormonal responses, and gene expression, among other systemic responses to stress. Note that the arrows from relationships to health are bidirectional: Healthy people promote good health, and healthy people are better able to foster positive relationships.

The context in which relationships are embedded – the sociocultural factors described in Chapter 1 that are upstream from the four socials – is not represented in Uchino's model, but it is inherent to our understanding of how relationships affect health and how health inequalities are perpetuated. These upstream factors, according to Berkman and colleagues, "condition the extent, shape, and nature of social networks."[2]

To be sure, the benefits of social relationships are not equally experienced by individuals across subgroups of the population. Most notably, a highly influential theory in social epidemiology, the Fundamental Cause Theory, suggests that socioeconomic status determines how social connections operate.[3] According to this theory, the stronger access to knowledge, resources, and beneficial social connections of high-status groups generally affords them to lead healthier lifestyles compared to low-status groups. Moreover, the social norms and other forms of social support among high-status groups promote and enable healthy lifestyles that are comparatively less available to lower-status groups.[4] In situating relationships within the broader context, we consider how they can have different impacts on wellbeing, behavior, and biological responses depending on socioeconomic status, race, and other societal factors. In the following sections detailing

[2] Berkman, L. F., Glass, T., Brissette, I., & Seeman, T. E. (2000). From social integration to health: Durkheim in the new millennium. *Social Science & Medicine* 51(6): 843–857. https://doi.org/10.1016/s0277-9536(00)00065-4.

[3] Link, B. G., & Phelan, J. (1995). Social conditions as fundamental causes of disease. *Journal of Health and Social Behavior*. https://doi.org/10.2307/2626958

[4] Phelan, J. C., Link, B. G., & Tehranifar, P. (2010). Social conditions as fundamental causes of health inequalities: theory, evidence, and policy implications. *Journal of Health and Social Behavior* 51 (Suppl. 1): S28–S40. https://doi.org/10.1177/0022146510383498

the research that addresses how the four socials are linked to health and how social relationships can be protective and also how they can have negative effects on health, the research that sheds light on these more upstream factors that shape relationship formation and maintenance are also examined.

Social Support

> We just don't have a roadmap for what we're currently experiencing – that in and of itself can bring up feelings of anxiety, loneliness, and fear . . . As for me, I know when I'm feeling overwhelmed that picking up the phone and calling one of my girlfriends can work wonders. I also know staying close to my community helps me to feel connected and strong.
>
> Michelle Obama, July 2020[5]

Social support includes the various types of care that people receive from others. Support can come in a variety of forms, and researchers generally agree on classifying these forms into three major categories:[6] emotional, instrumental, and informational support. *Emotional support* refers to the things that people do that make us feel loved and cared for and that bolster our sense of self-worth. When our friend helps us talk through a problem or our sister provides encouragement during a struggle at work, these are examples of emotional support. We might also consider these to be nontangible types of assistance. By contrast, *instrumental support* refers to the various types of tangible help that others may provide, such as a friend who helps drive you to the doctor or who picks up your kids when you are running late at work. *Informational support* refers to the help that others may offer through providing information, for example, the coworker who knows where you can get the best car service or where there might be a job opening.

Of the psychological pathway shown in Figure 2.1, social support has received the most attention from researchers. Social support protects health when a network of people is available and willing to give needed comfort and resources. We benefit from this support by feeling more positively about ourselves and perceiving our lives as having more

---

[5] CNN (2020). Michelle Obama has advice for Americans stuck indoors to help stem the spread of coronavirus. Retrieved from: www.cnn.com/2020/03/24/us/michelle-obama-coronavirus-message-americans-trnd/index.html.

[6] Richman, L. S. (2007). Life events & stress. In *The International Encyclopedia of the Social Sciences* (2nd ed.). MacMillan Reference.

meaning. These positive emotions are protective in and of themselves, but they can also promote better health maintenance – we take care of ourselves better when we are socially embedded. Support can promote positive psychological states, such as a sense of self-worth and purpose that induce health-promoting biological responses. Social support can also be a source of motivation and can influence how much we feel capable of pursuing goals we set for ourselves, such as maintaining healthy eating patterns or exercise programs.

Conversely, and unquestionably, relationships can also be *nonsupportive* and can be a source of psychological stress, such as when there is conflict and strain, and can increase risk for disease. Conflict and other undesirable social interactions can lead to negative evaluations of our self-worth and sense of belonging, thereby inducing long-term stress responses that are harmful to health.

In a series of studies, health psychologists examined the influence of social conflicts on susceptibility to the common cold.[7] They assessed whether research participants were involved in serious, enduring (one month or longer) social conflicts. They then exposed each participant to a virus that causes the common cold. Over the course of five days, researchers collected nasal secretion samples for virus culture and participants self-reported the presence and severity of any cold symptoms such as congestions, sore throat, and chills. They found that participants with enduring conflicts were more than twice as likely to develop a cold as people without chronic stressors in their lives. Other research has found that high negativity in spousal interactions can disrupt normal physiological functioning.[8] Couples who showed greater hostile behaviors during a thirty-minute discussion of marital problems had more negative immunological changes and larger increases in blood pressure that remained elevated for longer relative to low-hostility couples.

Strong support also enables us to cope with stressors in ways that reduce their toxicity. Social support can buffer the effect of stress on psychological distress, depression, and anxiety. The most damaging category of stress is the type that is unpredictable, uncontrollable, and chronic, which can be

[7] Cohen, S., Frank, E., Doyle, W. J., et al. (1998). Types of stressors that increase susceptibility to the common cold in healthy adults. *Health Psychology* 17(3): 214–223. https://doi.org/10.1037//0278-6133 .17.3.214; Cohen, S., Tyrrell, D. A. J., & Smith, A. P. (1991). Psychological stress and susceptibility to the common cold. *New England Journal of Medicine* 325: 606–612.

[8] Kiecolt-Glaser, J. K., Malarkey, W. B., Chee, M., & Newton, T. (1993). Negative behavior during marital conflict is associated with immunological down-regulation. *Psychosomatic Medicine* 55(5): 395–409.

particularly harmful as it activates stress responses that increase vulnerability to depression, substance use, and preclinical markers for cardiovascular disease. Turning to support networks is an important way in which people cope with interpersonal stressors. In studies where people are asked to indicate their perceived social support as well as the frequency with which they have experienced interpersonal discrimination, those with stronger social support are more buffered from experiencing depressive symptoms, a common response to discrimination experiences.[9]

Longitudinal studies that examine the effects of support in romantic relationships over time show that perceiving partner support for personal goals can be a powerful predictor of positive health outcomes. Support for personal goals, particularly by a close partner, increases successful achievement of those goals, which is especially beneficial when the goals are specifically health-relevant, such as abstaining from substance use.[10] Moreover, accomplishing goals we set for ourselves feels good and leads to greater wellbeing.

An interesting feature of social support is that even just the *perception* of how much of it we have can influence health. When researchers want to measure how much support someone has, they can ask about direct experiences, such as "Over the past week, how often did you confide in a friend or family member?" Or "How often did someone help you out with tasks around the house?" Alternatively, people can report on how they *perceive* the availability of support in their social network, rather than estimating the amount of support they actually received. The Interpersonal Support Evaluation List, or ISEL scale, is used to assess social support and includes questions about subjective, perceived support: "When I need suggestions on how to deal with a personal problem, I know someone I can turn to" and "It would be difficult to find someone to lend me their car for a few hours."[11] People who report that their networks are highly supportive are comparatively less likely to report health conditions such as obesity, anxiety, depression, and cardiovascular disease than those who lack strong support.[12] Perceptions of social

[9] Pascoe, E. A., & Richman, L. (2009). Perceived discrimination and health: a meta-analytic review. *Psychological Bulletin* 135(4): 531–554. https://doi.org/10.1037/a0016059

[10] Feeney, B. C., & Collins, N. L. (2015). A new look at social support: a theoretical perspective on thriving through relationships. *Personality and Social Psychology Review* 19(2): 113–147. https://doi.org/10.1177/1088868314544222

[11] Cohen, S., Mermelstein, R., Kamarck, T., & Hoberman, H. (1985). Measuring the functional components of social support. In I. G. Sarason & B. R. Sarason (Eds.), *Social Support: Theory, Research and Application* (pp. 73–94). Springer.

[12] Cadzow, R. B., & Servoss, T. J. (2009). The association between perceived social support and health among patients at a free urban clinic. *Journal of the National Medical Association* 101(3): 243–250. https://doi.org/10.1016/s0027-9684(15)30852

support can also affect prognosis when people are experiencing a particular health condition. For example, a review of research on perceived social support, loneliness, and depression found that people with depression who report low levels of perceived social support were more likely to have worse symptoms and recovery.

Most research on social support has thus far assumed that the support recipient is relatively passive and without much agency in shaping support outcomes. However, some psychological research has found that support recipients can cultivate effective support in a number of ways, including reaching out to others (vs. withdrawing), expressing needs clearly and directly, being receptive to others' support efforts, not placing too many demands on their social network, expressing gratitude, engaging in healthy dependence and independence, building a dense relationship network, and reciprocating support. Yet, the role of the support recipient in cultivating or hindering support processes is complex. Despite best intentions, many people have difficulty maintaining a supportive network, especially when people have health conditions that can limit their opportunities for socialization. Older adults may also experience challenges in maintaining strong social support after transitioning into retirement and the loss of family and friends. Furthermore, as described in Chapter 1, when people experience stigma based on their identities, such as with opioid use disorder, they may become socially withdrawn and be less able to seek out support opportunities. Chapter 6 explores how to cultivate support relationships.

The impact of social support on health is a dynamic process that plays out through the life course. Support from close family relationships as a child or adolescent can have lasting impacts on health. Emotional support from parents in childhood has been related to better health outcomes, whereas poor childhood family relationships, such as instances of abuse and parental marital conflict, have consistently been associated with adverse risk of health conditions as an adult. Life course perspectives on social support and health suggest that close childhood family relationships produce positive emotional and behavioral responses in children.[13] For example, stronger childhood family relationships can serve to cultivate prosocial interactional styles – that is, interactions with others that promote relationship building and continue with peers and partners into adulthood. Biologically, parenting styles may affect how the body regulates the release of the stress hormone cortisol by the hypothalamic–pituitary–adrenal (HPA) axis. Poor childhood

[13] Chen, E., Brody, G. H., & Miller, G. E. (2017). Childhood close family relationships and health. *The American Psychologist* 72(6): 555–566. https://doi.org/10.1037/amp0000067

relationships can lead to the dysregulation of this system, potentially affecting an individual's risk for chronic health conditions well into adulthood.

Certain sociocultural factors may affect how social support can impact health. For example, in more individualistic societies, such as the United States, a reliance on social support may be seen as detrimental to one's sense of self-worth, decreasing the likelihood of support-seeking. This is a different orientation than individuals from collectivist cultures, such as those found in much of Asia, where there is a higher value placed on social support and a frequent reliance on it for health promotion. For example, research that assessed attitudes of both Japanese and American participants found that Japanese participants reported a stronger inverse relationship between perceived social support and chronic ailments than American participants.[14]

The benefits of social support are limited by the extent to which it matches the needs of the one who receives it. Some evidence suggests that support can be most beneficial when it is unobtrusive and is consistent with what the receiver wants at the time. In contrast, unhelpful or unsolicited support may feel controlling, frustrate receivers, or make people feel less independent. Research has also started to consider the costs and benefits of providing social support, especially in the context of serving as a caregiver for a family member with chronic disease. An emerging literature explores how computer-mediated communication and online social networks can serve as valuable avenues to provide social support.[15]

Social Integration

Another pathway by which relationships may influence health status is by promoting social participation and social engagement. Social integration is a central concept of sociology. Developed by the French sociologist Emile Durkheim, it refers to the network of relationships and interactions – family, kinship groups, traditions, or economic activity – through which individuals are connected to each other to form a society. Getting together with friends, attending social functions, participating in occupations or social roles, engaging in group exercise, and attending religious rites are all instances of social engagement. Durkheim's seminal work in 1897 observed

---

[14] Park, J., Kitayama, S., Karasawa, M., et al. (2013). Clarifying the links between social support and health: culture, stress, and neuroticism matter. *Journal of Health Psychology* 18(2): 226–235. https://doi.org/10.1177/1359105312439731

[15] Kent de Grey, R., Uchino, B., Trettevik, R., Cronan, S., & Hogan, J. (2018). *Social Support*. Oxford University Press.

that social integration was an essential component of wellbeing, and that suicide was most prevalent among those who were neither married nor had close ties with the community and church.[16]

Social epidemiologists Lisa Berkman and Leonard Syme authored a modern classic of social integration research in 1979 that linked social relationships to mortality.[17] A random sample of almost 7,000 adults living in Alameda County, California were categorized into one of four levels on a "Social Network Index" – a composite measure that considered their cumulative number of social and community connections such as marriage status, contact with close relationships and friends, church membership, and informal and formal group associations.

In what was a profound set of findings at the time, the researchers reported that over a nine-year period, with each increasing level on the Social Network Index, the risk of death decreased. This relationship remained constant even when alternative explanations for mortality were considered, such as smoking, obesity, and use of preventive health services. In addition, Berkman and Syme found that social integration was protective not only for mortality, but also for a variety of other health conditions, such as heart disease, cancer, and cerebrovascular and circulatory diseases. At the time, this study presented some of the most compelling empirical links between social integration and mortality.

Most studies that examine the effects of social integration use the same or a similar measure that Berkman and Syme used in their original research. These social integration scales measure the number of recognized social positions, roles, or identities that people self-report, such as being a spouse, sister, friend, or church member. Numerous studies have built on and confirmed the Berkman and Syme research finding that socially integrated people live longer.[18] Other studies have found that greater integration predicts increased survival from heart attacks and less risk for metabolic dysregulation, less upper respiratory illness, less depression and anxiety, and less severe cognitive decline with aging.[19]

[16] Durkheim, E. (2013). *Suicide: A Study in Sociology.* Snowball Publishing.

[17] Berkman, L., & Syme, L. (1979). Social networks, host resistance, and mortality: a nine-year follow-up study of Alameda County residents. *American Journal of Epidemiology* 109(2): 186–204. https://doi.org/10.1093/oxfordjournals.aje.a112674

[18] House, J. S., Landis, K. R., & Umberson, D. (1988). Social relationships and health. *Science (New York, N.Y.)* 241(4865): 540–545. https://doi.org/10.1126/science.3399889. Uchino, B. N. (2004). *Social Support and Physical Health: Understanding the Health Consequences of Relationships* (pp. ix, 222). Yale University Press. https://doi.org/10.12987/yale/9780300102185.001.0001

[19] Berkman, L. F. (1995). The role of social relations in health promotion. *Psychosomatic Medicine* 57(3): 245–254. https://doi.org/10.1097/00006842-199505000-00006. Seeman, T. E. (1996). Social ties and

Other researchers have used creative ways to assess how social integration influences health outcomes. Using archival data from autobiographies of psychologists and literary writers, health psychologists counted words related to social ties (e.g., sister, neighbor, coworker) as well as words that referred to other individuals or interactions with others (e.g., they, us, friend, group, talk).[20] They found that greater use of words that were markers of social ties, other people, and interactions with others, was associated with living longer. For example, psychologists that most frequently mentioned social ties lived more than six years longer than those who mentioned it the least.

The protective health effects of social integration can be understood in several ways. Psychologically, as with social support, people who are more socially integrated tend to experience more positive emotions and have a stronger sense of identity and self-worth, which are all beneficial to health. Strong social networks can lead to a greater sense of belonging, with implications for improvements in mental health and health behaviors.[21] And also similar to the functions of social support, the biological association between social connectedness and various chronic diseases can also be explained by the buffering qualities of social connectedness against stress responses.[22] The more people are socially connected, the less likely they are to experience chronic stress and cumulative biological markers of stress. Although these findings are broadly applicable, certain factors, such as gender and socioeconomic status, as well as the quality and nature of the individual's social connections, often determine the extent to which social connectedness strengthens individual

health: the benefits of social integration. *Annals of Epidemiology* 6(5): 442–451. https://doi.org/10 .1016/s1047-2797(96)00095-6. Cohen, S., Doyle, W. J., Skoner, D. P., Rabin, B. S., & Gwaltney, J. M. (1997). Social ties and susceptibility to the common cold. *JAMA* 277(24): 1940–1944. Cohen, S., & Wills, T. A. (1985). Stress, social support, and the buffering hypothesis. *Psychological Bulletin* 98(2): 310–357. Kawachi, I., & Berkman, L. F. (2001). Social ties and mental health. *Journal of Urban Health: Bulletin of the New York Academy of Medicine* 78(3): 458–467. htt ps://doi.org/10.1093/jurban/78.3.458. Bassuk, S. S., Glass, T. A., & Berkman, L. F. (1999). Social disengagement and incident cognitive decline in community-dwelling elderly persons. *Annals of Internal Medicine* 131(3): 165–173. https://doi.org/10.7326/0003-4819-131-3-199908030-00002.

[20] Pressman, S. D., & Cohen, S. (2007). Use of social words in autobiographies and longevity. *Psychosomatic Medicine* 69(3): 262–269. https://doi.org/10.1097/PSY.0b013e31803cb919

[21] Sargent, J., Williams, R., Hagerty, B., Lynch-Sauer, J., & Hoyle, K. (2002). Sense of belonging as a buffer against depressive symptoms. *Journal of the American Psychiatric Nurses Association* 8: 120–129. https://doi.org/10.1067/mpn.2002.127290.

[22] Sonderlund, A. L., Thilsing, T., & Sondergaard, J. (2019). Should social disconnectedness be included in primary-care screening for cardiometabolic disease? A systematic review of the relationship between everyday stress, social connectedness, and allostatic load. *PLoS One* 14(12): e0226717. https://doi.org/10.1371/journal.pone.0226717

resilience to stress. Men, for example, appear to benefit more from spousal and parental ties as well as from general social connectedness than women do, whereas women seem to benefit more than men from friendships and general family relationships.

Behaviorally, social integration can also confer health benefits by affecting responsiveness to the social influence of others.[23] When people have high levels of social integration there is more opportunity to be subject to social controls and peer pressures that promote positive health behaviors such as exercise, better diet, not smoking, and moderating alcohol intake. Having conversations with other parents at your children's school, at religious gatherings, or with neighbors all provide these opportunities. Being socially integrated, especially with a wide range of network ties, increases the probability of gaining access to information that can facilitate healthy behaviors and assist in avoiding stressful or high-risk situations. When people are embedded in a social network they are also more motivated to care for themselves and social integration is associated with patients' adherence to medical regimens.[24]

Interestingly, although peer influence can certainly lead to negative health behaviors, the association between social integration and social influence seems to be primarily a positive influence. A study by health psychologists Sheldon Cohen and Edward Lemay examined the relation between social integration, emotions, and smoking and alcohol consumption. They administered social integration and psychological questionnaires to 193 adults and then interviewed them for fourteen consecutive evenings about their daily social interactions, emotions, and health behaviors. Their findings are intriguing, although perhaps counter-intuitive at first glance. They found that higher social integration scores were associated with consuming fewer alcoholic drinks and smoking fewer cigarettes over the fourteen-day study period. Whether people derived happiness or negative emotion from these interactions did not seem to play a role in their health behaviors. Rather, the authors conclude that greater social integration leads to more social pressure from the network to stay healthy and by inducing greater responsibility to others. Social integration seems to influence how people react to their social environment. Where those low in social integration showed a susceptibility to moment-by-moment social pressures that influence their behaviors, those with higher social

[23] Cohen, S., & Lemay, E. P. (2007). Why would social networks be linked to affect and health practices? *Health Psychology* 26(4): 410–417. https://doi.org/10.1037/0278-6133.26.4.410

[24] DiMatteo, M. R. (2004). Social support and patient adherence to medical treatment: a meta-analysis. *Health Psychology* 23(2): 207–218. https://doi.org/10.1037/0278-6133.23.2.207

integration had health behaviors that were relatively independent of the number of interaction partners over the study period. These findings have compelling implications that more socially integrated people are responsive to the ongoing normative constraints of living a healthy lifestyle.

Moreover, various kinds of social integration influence health outcomes differently and the macro, social structure and context play an important role in determining how able people may be to shape the networks in which they are embedded. Certain types of social integration will lend themselves to good health (e.g., gardening clubs) and others to bad health (e.g., street gangs) and the social structural conditions that shape these networks are important to understand. People will be most likely to achieve positive health outcomes and thrive both emotionally and physically when they are embedded in a network of responsive relationships with friends, siblings, intimate partners, parents, mentors, and others who together serve important support functions.[25] For example, having close, meaningful relationships with diverse social network members is a stronger predictor of mortality than are measures of marital status or network size.[26] The positive aspects of social ties have been the main focus of research attention, particularly in regard to protective health effects and longevity, but our social ties can also bring conflict, exploitation, and stress. Programs that incorporate relationship principles into health care delivery must appreciate this duality. Avoiding draining or harmful social ties needs to be prioritized in addition to strengthening helpful social ties.

Social Capital

Social relationships affect our health not just from *how much* people interact with others in their network, but also *who* these people are, and *what* they can offer as a result of connections to them – that is, our *social capital*. In its broadest form, social capital refers to the quantity and quality of resources that we have access to through our social connections. Social capital research has demonstrated relationships between neighborhood or community characteristics and life expectancy, health and wellbeing,

[25] Feeney, B. C., & Collins, N. L. (2014). A theoretical perspective on the importance of social connections for thriving. In M. Mikulincer & P. Shaver (Eds.), *Mechanisms of Social Connection: from Brain to Group* (pp. 291–314). American Psychological Association. https://doi.org/10.1037/14 250-017

[26] Feeney, B. C., & Collins, N. L. (2015). New look at social support: a theoretical perspective on thriving through relationships. *Personality and Social Psychology Review* 19(2): 113–147. https://doi .org/10.1177/1088868314544222

health care access, and health behaviors.[27] Social capital has been linked to health outcomes in a variety of settings, including neighborhoods, workplaces, and schools.[28] Having a diversity of network ties provides multiple sources of information that could influence health-related behaviors, lead to more effective use of available health services, or help avoid stressful or high-risk situations.

Although social capital can be a means to gain important health information or access to better care, it can also exacerbate inequality. People with limited social resources have fewer opportunities to develop social capital, chiefly because individuals generally have social networks composed of people who have similar socioeconomic backgrounds. Generally, high socioeconomic status confers more opportunities to get the types of social support that benefit health, whereas the broader social networks of people with low socioeconomic status may have similar limited access to health-conferring resources (transportation, information, financial support, etc.) and thus may not be able to provide the levels of support that may be needed.

Social capital has been distinguished into two types – bonding and bridging – which are useful concepts to clarify how social capital can differentially benefit people. These are not the only types of social capital that have been defined and examined in this literature, but they are arguably the most fundamental to understanding how social capital affects health outcomes. Bonding social capital has been defined as the connections between members of a network that are similar to each other with respect to social class, race/ethnicity, or other attributes. Bridging social capital is defined as the connections between people who are dissimilar with respect to socioeconomic status and other characteristics.[29] Figure 2.2 illustrates how both of these types of social capital can connect two communities.

Social epidemiologists emphasize that the distinction between these types of social capital is important because reciprocal exchanges that can take place in groups with high bonding social capital are constrained by the amounts of

[27] Lindström, B., Röding, J., & Sundelin, G. (2009). Positive attitudes and preserved high level of motor performance are important factors for return to work in younger persons after stroke: a national survey. *Journal of Rehabilitation Medicine* 41(9): 714–718. https://doi.org/10.2340/165019 77-0423

[28] Villalonga-Olives, E., Adams, I., & Kawachi, I. (2016). The development of a bridging social capital questionnaire for use in population health research. *SSM – Population Health* 2: 613–622. https://doi.org/10.1016/j.ssmph.2016.08.008

[29] Villalonga-Olives, E., Adams, I., & Kawachi, I. (2016). The development of a bridging social capital questionnaire for use in population health research. *SSM – Population Health* 2: 613–622. https://doi.org/10.1016/j.ssmph.2016.08.008

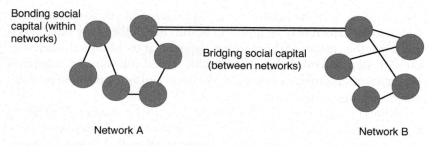

Bonding social capital (within networks)

Bridging social capital (between networks)

Network A   Network B

Figure 2.2 How social capital connects two communities. Modified from Adams.[30]

resources available within the network. For example, as referenced in the earlier review of social support, the social ties that exist within socioeconomically disadvantaged communities may be characterized by intense levels of mutual assistance, but the overall availability of resources (e.g., cash loans) is often constrained. Therefore, bonding social capital in these circumstances, "community-rich, but resource-poor," can actually strain the psychosocial wellbeing of network members by frequent demands and unmet needs. Bridging social capital, in contrast, enables low-resourced people to gain access to valued resources, such as connections to job opportunities or information, that they may be disconnected from in their own communities. This ability to access resources from outside one's own network has been associated with better health outcomes, and particularly with better mental health.[31]

In an analysis of the effects of bonding and bridging social capital in forty US communities, researchers at the Harvard School of Public Health found that both types of social capital afforded modest protection for self-rated health.[32] In a sampling strategy that was designed to broadly represent the diversity of communities across the country, they found that in response to the questions, "How would you describe your overall state of health these days? Would you say it is excellent, very good, good, fair, or poor?" communities with higher social capital (of both types) had relatively higher self-rated health as compared with communities with lower social

[30] Adams, C. (2020). Toward an institutional perspective on social capital health interventions: lay community health workers as social capital builders. *Sociology of Health and Illness* 42: 95–110. https://doi.org/10.1111/1467-9566.12992

[31] Mitchell, C. U., & LaGory, M. (2002). Social capital and mental distress in an impoverished community. *City & Community* 1(2): 199–222. https://doi.org/10.1111/1540-6040.00017

[32] Kim, D., Subramanian, S. V., & Kawachi, I. (2006). Bonding versus bridging social capital and their associations with self rated health: a multilevel analysis of 40 US communities. *Journal of Epidemiology and Community Health* 60(2): 116–122. https://doi.org/10.1136/jech.2005.038281

capital. More work is needed to better understand the mechanisms by which social capital may be linked to health, but of the many functions it can serve, the authors of this research suggest that social capital accelerates the diffusion of knowledge about health-related innovations, maintains health norms, promotes access to local services and amenities, and provides emotional support and mutual respect.

Figure 2.3 illustrates how social capital can be measured, showing examples from a scale developed by epidemiologists Villalonga-Olives, Adams, and Kawachi to measure bridging social capital in Latino immigrant populations in the United States. For this assessment tool, participants are asked to respond to the frequency of different kinds of socializing behavior (never to very often) and the availability of people who they felt they could turn to as sources of information (yes or no responses).

The concept of social capital contributes to an understanding of both the capacities and limitations of social networks for improving health and

---

How often do you socialize (i.e. go out for drinks, visit each other's homes) with co-workers who ...

(a) *Are of a different nationality?*

(b) *Speak a different language?*

(c) *Are from a different race/ethnic background than you?*

(d) *Have different political opinions?*

(e) *Have a different level of education?*

Do you know anyone in your life who can assist you with the following kinds of situations?

1. *Can give advice on matters of law (e.g. problems with landlord, boss).*

2. *Provide advice about local schools.*

3. *Can write a good reference/recommendation letter when you are applying for a job.*

Figure 2.3 Questions about bridging social capital. From Villalonga-Olives et al.[33]

[33] Villalonga-Olives et al., The development of a bridging social capital questionnaire.

wellbeing. It also offers insights into how interventions to promote community development and community health might address the needs of groups with limited social capital. This research suggests that intervention efforts that aim to improve resource opportunities most likely need to be focused on bridged social capital, which has the capacity to enable better access to valued resources and information embedded within them.

Social Norms

The importance of social relationships to health and wellbeing has also been captured in the construct of social norms. Social networks are subject to social controls and peer pressures that influence normative health behaviors. These "social norms" generally refer to codes of conduct in ways of thinking and behaving and thereby provide an unspoken agreement to conform to certain actions and behaviors. Social norms are pervasive in health behaviors, and an individual's perception of social norms are powerful predictors of engagement with various health-related factors. When such behavior is a norm, acceptance in the group is tied to following the established norm, and violation of the norm creates social friction. Adjusting behavior to perceived group norms can encourage health-promoting behaviors, but it can also work to encourage unhealthy ones.

An emerging area of research focuses on how perceptions of social norms affect population health. Social norms provide an efficient way to interact, a set of ground rules for behavior, and a set of sanctions when broken. Perceptions of norms are most likely to lead to behavioral changes when certain conditions are met. These include: (1) individuals identify with the source of information; (2) norms are considered believable; (3) personal views align with the norm; (4) the norm is well known; and/or (5) norms are contextualized.[34] Under these conditions, perceptions of norms can impact healthy behaviors by providing social motivation and promoting behaviors that are not always publicly observable. For example, perceptions of norms can influence decisions on whether to exercise, what to eat, and whether to undergo routine medical screenings. Social norms can be difficult to study specifically because they are often unseen and ubiquitous.

Social comparisons can often influence both what people perceive to be applicable social norms and their motivations for behavior change. The

---

[34] Tankard, M. E., & Paluck, E. L. (2016). Norm perception as a vehicle for social change. *Social Issues and Policy Review* 10(1): 181–211. https://doi.org/10.1111/sipr.12022

challenge is that people's perceptions of where they stand are vulnerable to systematic biases and errors, usually by overestimating the amount we engage in healthy behaviors and underestimating the amount we engage in unhealthy behaviors compared to others.[35] In one research study demonstrating this bias, participants were given the instructions, "Assume there are 99 other people in the study, and we ordered them according to how often they eat junk food. Slide the scale to indicate where you place among 99 other people in the study. I eat junk food more than __ of the other people in the study." Participants tended to misjudge their comparative standing to their fellow university students for a variety of health-relevant behaviors, showing a favorability bias. Estimates tended to be too high for the healthy behaviors (averaging significantly above the 50th percentile) and too low for unhealthy ones. In addition, they found that the people who engaged in the most unhealthy behaviors also tended to be the most inaccurate in estimating their social comparative standing. This estimation bias can hamper health-promoting behaviors because the people who most need to change their behaviors might be the least likely to recognize this need.[36]

Social norms heavily influence the attitudes and behaviors of adolescents and young adults on substance abuse, and thus social norm measures are used in most health behavior models that predict risky health behaviors, including substance use (e.g., the Theory of Planned Behavior, Prototype Willingness Model).[37] These measures are typically divided into *descriptive* or *injunctive* norms. Descriptive norms are people's perceptions of what others are doing. For example, college students might be asked: "What percentage of students at your college regularly use e-cigarettes?" or "How many of your close friends use marijuana?" Injunctive norms are perceptions of others' approval or disapproval of engagement in the behavior norms. When measuring perceived approval, students might be asked: "If I were to regularly use e-cigarettes my close friends would approve" or "If I were to use marijuana my parents would disapprove." Each of these questions would be

[35] Gerber, J. P., Wheeler, L., & Suls, J. (2018). A social comparison theory meta-analysis 60+ years on. *Psychological Bulletin* 144(2): 177–197. https://doi.org/10.1037/bul0000127

[36] Miller, J. E., Windschitl, P. D., Treat, T. A., & Scherer, A. M. (2019). Unhealthy and unaware? Misjudging social comparative standing for health-relevant behavior. *Journal of Experimental Social Psychology* 85: 103873. https://doi.org/10.1016/j.jesp.2019.103873

[37] Ajzen, I. (1991). The theory of planned behavior. *Organizational Behavior and Human Decision Processes* 50(2): 179–211. https://doi.org/10.1016/0749-5978(91)90020-T. Gerrard, M., Gibbons, F. X., Houlihan, A. E., Stock, M. L., & Pomery, E. A. (2008). A dual-process approach to health risk decision making: the prototype willingness model. *Developmental Review* 28(1): 29–61. https://doi.org/10.1016/j.dr.2007.10.001

followed by a scale (e.g., 1 = strongly disagree to 5 = strongly agree). For both descriptive and injunctive norms the reference group (from which the normative information comes – e.g., other students, close friends, parents) plays an important role. In general, both types of norms have been shown to be associated with and predictive of substance use behaviors, including alcohol,[38] marijuana, hard drugs, nonmedical stimulants, performance-enhancing substances, and e-cigarette use.[39] In addition, perceived norms based on media (e.g., exposure to popular movies) and social networking sites (such as Facebook) are also predictive of substance use behaviors. Youth who are exposed more to substance use behaviors and messages through movies, shows, advertisements, and social media see substance use behaviors as more normative and are at higher risk for future substance use. Making people aware of the descriptive norms of certain unhealthy behaviors, such as alcohol consumption, has been successful as an intervention in reducing the frequency of engagement in those behaviors.[40]

The research on social norms suggests why information-based programs that are designed to improve knowledge about health

---

[38] Neighbors, C., LaBrie, J. W., Hummer, J. F., et al. (2010). Group identification as a moderator of the relationship between perceived social norms and alcohol consumption. *Psychology of Addictive Behaviors* 24(3): 522–528. https://doi.org/10.1037/a0019944

[39] Pedersen, E. R., Osilla, K. C., Miles, J. N. V., et al. (2017). The role of perceived injunctive alcohol norms in adolescent drinking behavior. *Addictive Behaviors* 67: 1–7. https://doi.org/10.1016/j.addbeh.2016.11.022. Ellickson, P. L., Tucker, J. S., Klein, D. J., & Saner, H. (2004). Antecedents and outcomes of marijuana use initiation during adolescence. *Preventive Medicine: An International Journal Devoted to Practice and Theory* 39(5): 976–984. https://doi.org/10.1016/j.ypmed.2004.04.013. Mahalik, J. R., Lombardi, C. M., Sims, J., Coley, R. L., & Lynch, A. D. (2015). Gender, male-typicality, and social norms predicting adolescent alcohol intoxication and marijuana use. *Social Science & Medicine* 143: 71–80. https://doi.org/10.1016/j.socscimed.2015.08.013. Barman-Adhikari, A., Craddock, J., Bowen, E., Das, R., & Rice, E. (2018). The relative influence of injunctive and descriptive social norms on methamphetamine, heroin, and injection drug use among homeless youths: the impact of different referent groups. *Journal of Drug Issues* 48(1): 17–35. https://doi.org/10.1177/0022042617726080. Bavarian, N., Flay, B. R., Ketcham, P. L., & Smit, E. (2015). The illicit use of prescription stimulants on college campuses: a theory-guided systematic review. *Health Education & Behavior* 42(6): 719–729. https://doi.org/10.1177/1090198115580576. Scheinfeld, E., Crook, B., & Perry, C. L. (2019). Understanding young adults' e-cigarette use through the theory of planned behavior. *Health Behavior and Policy Review* 6(2): 115–127. https://doi.org/10.14485/hbpr.6.2.1. Jackson, K. M., Janssen, T., & Gabrielli, J. (2018). Media/marketing influences on adolescent and young adult substance abuse. *Current Addiction Reports* 5(2): 146–157. https://doi.org/10.1007/s40429-018-0199-6. Groth, G. G., Longo, L. M., & Martin, J. L. (2017). Social media and college student risk behaviors: a mini-review. *Addictive Behaviors* 65: 87–91. https://doi.org/10.1016/j.addbeh.2016.10.00. Nesi, J., Rothenberg, W. A., Hussong, A. M., & Jackson, K. M. (2017). Friends' alcohol-related social networking site activity predicts escalations in adolescent drinking: mediation by peer norms. *Journal of Adolescent Health: Official Publication of the Society for Adolescent Medicine* 60(6): 641–647. https://doi.org/10.1016/j.jadohealth.2017.01.009

[40] Ridout, B., & Campbell, A. (2014). Using Facebook to deliver a social norm intervention to reduce problem drinking at university. *Drug and Alcohol Review* 33(6): 667–673. https://doi.org/10.1111/dar.12141

behaviors often fail to change behavior. One factor contributing to poor compliance is that in order to successfully engage individuals in health promotion, the health behavior needs to feel culturally relevant, a norm for the groups to which people identify. Historically, racial and ethnic minorities have been underrepresented in health promotion advertising and marketing campaigns, and that underrepresentation has served to shape what is norm-defining for certain groups. Interventions aimed at decreasing racial disparities in health could benefit from using culturally tailored messages to increase perceived relevance of health promotion behaviors.[41]

The Role of Social Disconnection

The COVID-19 pandemic has provided a sort of natural experiment to examine pervasive effects of a prolonged curtailment of the typical functions of our social networks. Available research suggests that the COVID-19 pandemic reduced social contact for everyone and completely isolated many, significantly increasing rates of distress and poor mental health. Obesity and substance use have also seen sharp increases during this time. In a survey of US adults conducted by the American Psychological Association in late February 2021, 42 percent experienced undesired weight gain, exhibiting average gains of twenty-nine pounds, and 10 percent reported gaining more than fifty pounds.[42] Social isolation has led to greater rates of substance use and overdose, with every state showing a spike or increase in overdose deaths during COVID-19.[43] These are only immediate impacts of the pandemic on health and health behaviors, and the suspected long-term effects may be even more concerning.

Even prior to COVID-19-imposed isolation, some of the strongest evidence for the profound influences of social relationships on health came from research that examined what happens to people when they are chronically *lacking* in supportive social relationships. Chronic social

[41] Oyserman, D., Novin, S., Flinkenflögel, N., & Krabbendam, L. (2014). Integrating culture-as-situated-cognition and neuroscience prediction models. *Culture and Brain* 2(1): 1–26. https://doi.org/10.1007/s40167-014-0016-6

[42] Bethune, S. (2021). One year on: unhealthy weight gains, increased drinking reported by Americans coping with pandemic stress. American Psychology Association. Retrieved from: www.apa.org/news/press/releases/2021/03/one-year-pandemic-stress.

[43] American Medical Association Advocacy Resource Center (2021). Issue brief: Nation's drug-related overdose and death epidemic continues to worsen. Retrieved from: www.ama-assn.org/system/files/issue-brief-increases-in-opioid-related-overdose.pdf.

isolation and loneliness contribute to poor health and even premature death. Social isolation, a circumstance that is characterized by extremely limited social contact, can stem from being rejected or excluded from relationships and groups, but it can also develop as a consequence of winnowing social networks with old age. Many health costs are associated with social isolation and feelings of loneliness, which is a subjective feeling of isolation that is correlated with, but not necessarily the same thing as, the lack of close connections.

Isolation and loneliness are both related to worse physical and mental functioning and premature death,[44] and have proven to be robust predictors of adverse outcomes in the context of cardiovascular, respiratory, and infectious diseases, as well as certain cancers. In fact, social isolation is as strong a predictor of mortality as smoking and high blood pressure.[45] Certain groups may be particularly at risk for social isolation. The effects of social isolation have dire consequences for the health of mothers and their families. The 2017 New York City Vital Signs report indicates that women are more likely to experience postpartum depressive symptoms (PDS) when they have less social support,[46] and PDS is associated with worse cognitive and physical outcomes for children. In their survey, 15 percent of women reported one or no relationships to whom they could turn in a time of need. Women also tend to be primary caregivers later in life and are at particular risk for social isolation and depression during this life stage.

Conclusions

The "four socials" of social support, social integration, social capital, and social norms play an influential role in shaping health outcomes through psychological, behavioral, and biological pathways. Higher levels of perceived social support, social integration, social capital (bridging social capital in particular), and positive social norms all serve to promote healthy behaviors and outcomes. Personal relationships, such as friendships and romantic partnerships, as well as social institutions such as family, religion,

---

[44] Hawkley, L. C., & Cacioppo, J. T. (2003). Loneliness and pathways to disease. *Brain, Behavior, and Immunity* 17(Suppl. 1): S98–S105. https://doi.org/10.1016/s0889-1591(02)00073-9

[45] Pantell, M., Rehkopf, D., Jutte, D., Syme, S. L., Balmes, J., & Adler, N. (2013). Social isolation: A predictor of mortality comparable to traditional clinical risk factors. *American Journal of Public Health* 103(11): 2056–2062. https://doi.org/10.2105/AJPH.2013.301261

[46] Negron, R., Martin, A., Almog, M., Balbierz, A., & Howell, E. A. (2013). Social support during the postpartum period: mothers' views on needs, expectations, and mobilization of support. *Maternal and Child Health Journal* 17(4): 616–623. https://doi.org/10.1007/s10995-012-1037-4

and schools are common sources of relationship development and influence. At the same time, disconnection and negative relational influences, such as peer pressure or unhealthy social norms, can contribute to the development and sustainability of these health issues and are also essential to consider.

CHAPTER 3

The Relationship-Driven Factors in Obesity, Opioid Use Disorder, and Depression in Older Adults

---

Key Points

- Social networks affect the spread and prevalence of obesity. Social support from family and close relationships and community norms can promote dietary health, whereas weight stigma can contribute to weight gain.
- The development of addiction is marked by impaired relational functioning as well as physiological changes. Social norms among peer groups and low social integration are also critical contributors to misuse.
- Age-related changes can pose challenges to maintaining social relationships and can increase risk of loneliness, social isolation, and depression in older adults.

Introduction

This chapter examines how the relationship factors described in Chapter 2 influence three major health concerns – obesity, opioid use disorder, and depression among older adults. These are complex health concerns, and each is heavily influenced by multiple relational factors that can increase risk or be protective. A goal of the relational health approach is to incorporate the scientific evidence for how relationships affect these health issues and how they might help those suffering from them. These relational aspects are vital missing pieces in how we think about and provide care for people who grapple with these health issues.

The Case of Obesity

What I want you to understand, more than anything else, is that telling a fat person "Eat less and exercise" is like telling a boxer "Don't get hit." You act as if there's not an opponent. Losing weight is a fucking rock fight. The enemies come from all sides. The deluge of marketing telling us to eat worse and eat more. The culture that has turned food into one of the last acceptable vices. Our families and friends who want us to share in their pleasure. Our own body chemistry, dragging us back to the table out of fear that we'll starve. On top of that, some of us fight holes in our souls that a boxcar of doughnuts couldn't fill.

Tommy Tomlinson, *Elephant in the Room*, p. 137[1]

In the book, *Elephant in the Room*, a journalist writes eloquently about his lifelong struggles with his weight. He describes grappling with a culture that both shuns him for his weight and actively contributes to his unwanted weight gain. Being a person with obesity or overweight has a value attached to it, quite literally, in which calculations are based on measures of weight and height – body mass index (BMI) – and are determined to be within the spectrum of unhealthy weight. Approximately 40 percent of American adults currently live with obesity and another one-third are overweight and at risk for obesity. Researchers at Harvard published a study in the *New England Journal of Medicine* estimating that, given current trends, by 2030 nearly one in two adults nationwide will have obesity and approximately one in four will have severe obesity.[2]

The terms "obesity" and "overweight" are frequently used interchangeably to describe the condition of excess weight, but in a health context they are distinguished using the BMI index definitions. The distinction between obesity and overweight is important clinically for identifying health risks. Obesity, but not overweight, is a chronic disease that can lead to complications that impact mental and physical functioning, quality of life, and can reduce life expectancy. Obesity-related conditions such as cardiovascular disease, certain cancers, and diabetes are among the leading causes of preventable death in this country. The distinction between these terms is less important, however, for understanding the relational aspects that contribute to and can be leveraged to address excess weight;[3] these aspects are similar across the spectrum from overweight to obesity. Obesity

---

[1] Tomlinson, T. (2019). *The Elephant in the Room: One Fat Man's Quest to Get Smaller in a Growing America*. Simon & Schuster.

[2] Ward, Z. J., Bleich, S. N., Cradock, A. L., et al. (2019). Projected U.S. state-level prevalence of adult obesity and severe obesity. *New England Journal of Medicine* 381(25): 2440–2450. https://doi.org/10.1056/NEJMsa1909301

[3] Puhl, R. M., & Brownell, K. D. (2003). Psychosocial origins of obesity stigma: toward changing a powerful and pervasive bias. *Obesity Reviews* 4(4): 213–227. https://doi.org/10.1046/j.1467-789X.2003.00122.x

will be the term used throughout this chapter to describe the condition of having a weight that is a risk factor for numerous poor health outcome, rather than representing a specific BMI cutoff.

Drivers of Risk of Obesity

As Tomlinson details in his memoir, many factors influence our weight, but as individuals we have control over only a small fraction of them. Although our weight is determined by so-called "controllable" behaviors, such as whether we consume excess calories and the amount of exercise we do (although the science is increasingly suggesting that exercise plays a smaller role influencing weight than once thought), our weight is also determined by many "uncontrollable" factors that are biological, such as the genes we inherit, our endocrine function, and the way our metabolism works. Our mental state (including depression, stress, and anxiety) as well as environmental factors (including access to healthy foods or energy-dense foods, targeted marketing, and safe walking spaces in our neighborhoods) all play a role in determining our weight.

Major public efforts have been directed toward changing the "obesogenic environments" that have become all too common for many communities in the United States.[4] To live in an "obesogenic" environment means that you are inescapably surrounded by contributors to unhealthy weight gain that constrain options and shape social norms around consumption. These obesogenic environments are widespread and tend to cluster in high-poverty neighborhoods where the quickest, cheapest, and often the only food options are those that are highly processed and excessively caloric. Obesogenic environments provide limited opportunities for regular access to healthy foods as well as exercise. Residents of these areas are also disproportionately exposed to advertising for sugary drinks and other high caloric and low nutritional value foods targeting children. This media barrage has been shown to have lifelong implications for tastes, preferences, and consumption patterns.

These environmental factors help to explain how high-poverty areas also have higher rates of obesity. Typically, researchers who are interested in examining environmental influences on behaviors and health are limited to observational studies. This type of research design can reveal associations between exposures and outcomes, but they cannot reliably establish causality. Researchers can, for example, examine how the number of billboards in a neighborhood that advertise sugary beverages is associated with rates of

---

[4] Lakerveld, J., & Mackenbach, J. (2017). The upstream determinants of adult obesity. *Obesity Facts* 10: 216–222. https://doi.org/10.1159/000471489

obesity. The effects of exposure to these advertisements can also be examined over time, whereby researchers measure how a neighborhood's exposure to advertisements can predict obesity over a specified time period, taking initial health into account. These kinds of studies can show important associations between environmental characteristics and obesity, but they cannot show whether an observed effect is due to aspects of the environment (advertisements in this case) that cause an outcome (obesity). Any relationship could result from an unmeasured or poorly measured third variable that could affect both exposure and obesity. For this example, maybe neighborhoods with high numbers of sugary beverage advertisements also tend to have fewer alternative beverage options in local stores. In order to draw causal conclusions, people would need to be randomly assigned to certain conditions and then compared to those who are exposed to different conditions. This kind of study design, called the randomized controlled trial (RCT), is the most powerful research design to draw causal conclusions. However, since it is both infeasible and unethical to randomly assign people to environmental conditions over time that are suspected to be harmful to health, researchers must resort to other methodologies.

Sometimes government programs offer rare opportunities to examine effects of different conditions based on fortuitous random assignment. In 1994, the US Department of Housing and Urban Development (HUD) launched the Moving to Opportunity (MTO) program, in which it enrolled 4,604 low-income public housing families living in high-poverty neighborhoods within five US cities: Baltimore, Boston, Chicago, Los Angeles, and New York. Through a lottery, families were randomly assigned into one of three groups. The low-poverty voucher group was composed of families who received housing vouchers that could only be used in census tracts with 1990 poverty rates below 10 percent. The traditional voucher group received regular Section 8 housing vouchers without any relocation constraint. Finally, a control group was composed of families who remained in public housing and receive no additional assistance through MTO. Due to this random assignment, MTO provided a unique opportunity to isolate the effects of neighborhood on the lives of low-income families.

A 2011 study took advantage of this unique opportunity to examine whether neighborhood environments contribute directly to the development of obesity.[5] From 2008 through 2010, the researchers measured participants'

[5] Ludwig, J., Sanbonmatsu, L., Gennetian, L., et al. (2011). Neighborhoods, obesity, and diabetes: a randomized social experiment. *New England Journal of Medicine* 365(16): 1509–1519. https://doi.org /10.1056/NEJMsa1103216

health outcomes, including BMI and level of glycated hemoglobin, a biomarker for diabetes. The results showed that the group with a randomly assigned opportunity to use a voucher to move to a neighborhood with a lower poverty rate had a lower prevalence of obesity than the control group, whereas the group receiving traditional vouchers exhibited no significant weight difference from the control group. The authors provided the following summary of their results: "The findings show that the opportunity to move from a neighborhood with a high level of poverty to one with a lower level of poverty was associated with modest, but potentially important, reductions in the prevalence of obesity and diabetes." The characteristics of obesogenic environments is one level by which risk for obesity increases. Access to healthy food, opportunities to exercise, and exposure to target marketing for unhealthy products can constrain choices and have significant influences on consumption patterns and weight gain.

Our relationships also influence our dietary patterns in important ways, both contributing to risk factors for obesity and insulating us from these risks. What are often viewed as individual dietary choices and behaviors are, in actuality, highly influenced by those around us. These relational factors – the myriad ways in which our social relationships and the environments in which they are embedded – interact with both the controllable and uncontrollable factors to impact behaviors and outcomes.

As described in Chapter 1, our relationships are shaped by and exist within particular social-structural conditions. The characteristics of our social networks provide opportunities to reap the benefits of our social relationships and also be impacted by unhealthy norms. This point can be observed most clearly in the "social clustering" of obesity, which is a term used to describe how we are more likely to have a body weight that is similar to that of other people in our social network. The importance of social networks – real and virtual – in obesity development is a relatively new area of research that capitalizes on known characteristics of infectious disease transmission. In a landmark 2007 study examining the spread of obesity due to social ties using thirty-two-year prospective data from the Framingham Heart Study, epidemiologists Christakis and Fowler showed that an individual's likelihood of becoming obese increased by 57 percent if they had a friend who became obese in a given four-year interval.[6] Other studies have found that people who are overweight have more social ties

[6] Christakis, N. A., & Fowler, J. H. (2007). The spread of obesity in a large social network over 32 years. *New England Journal of Medicine* 357(4): 370–379. https://doi.org/10.1056/NEJMsa066082

that are also overweight, and that spouses, siblings, and friends have concordant food choices and become more alike in weight status over time.

Certain features of social networks have been shown to have important influences on weight status. For example, in an adult sample in Montreal that was followed for over five years, researchers found that having higher levels of trust in your neighbors (higher "bonding" social capital) was associated with lower risk of an individual becoming obese.[7] These higher levels of interpersonal trust between neighbors can increase openness toward health-promoting messages and innovations in a community. In addition, this same study found that those individuals who had greater network diversity (higher "bridging" social capital) were less likely to be obese over the five-year period than those without that diversity. In short, when we have greater variety within our social networks, we gain certain benefits, which include access to a broader range of information and resources that can improve dietary behavior and other preventive health opportunities – all factors that can operate indirectly to reduce the risk of obesity. Other work has found similar results that show how network diversity achieved through depth and breadth of involvement in volunteer work corresponds to a lower likelihood of being overweight.[8]

Social norms are another relational factor that play an important role in weight control behavior. Culture, family, friends, and peers all contribute to creating social norms and role modeling behaviors. When people are connected with others who actively participate in weight control behaviors, they have greater exposure to (and more likelihood of applying) the information, modeling, and social norms that are established and promoted within the social network.[9] Having a large proportion of social ties to people who engage in physical activity or particular eating behaviors may make these behaviors "normative" and lead to pressure to conform. In studies of young adults, having a higher number of social contacts who exercise regularly reduces the likelihood of physical inactivity.[10]

[7] Wu, Y.-H., Moore, S., & Dube, L. (2018). Social capital and obesity among adults: longitudinal findings from the Montreal Neighborhood Networks and Healthy Aging Panel. *Preventive Medicine* 111: 366–370. https://doi.org/10.1016/j.ypmed.2017.11.028

[8] Veenstra, G., Luginaah, I., Wakefield, S., et al. (2005). Who you know, where you live: social capital, neighbourhood and health. *Social Science & Medicine (1982)* 60(12): 2799–2818. https://doi.org/10.1016/j.socscimed.2004.11.013

[9] Leahey, T. M., LaRose, J. G., Fava, J. L., & Wing, R. R. (2011). Social influences are associated with BMI and weight loss intentions in young adults. *Obesity* 19(6): 1157–1162. https://doi.org/10.1038/oby.2010.301

[10] Leroux, J. S., Moore, S., Richard, L., & Gauvin, L. (2012). Physical inactivity mediates the association between the perceived exercising behavior of social network members and obesity: a cross-sectional study. *PLoS One* 7(10): e46558. https://doi.org/10.1371/journal.pone.0046558

The behaviors of those in our social networks may play an especially important role in the weight changes of women. In a study of weight and weight control behaviors of Latinas and their social ties, Dr. Becky Marquez and colleagues at the University of San Diego and University of Connecticut studied a large sample of overweight and inactive women who resided in San Diego County.[11] This study collected data using a name generator where each participant provided names of people with whom she discussed important matters in the past year and to rank order the names according to whom they felt the most to least close. Information was collected for each social tie such as age, gender, ethnicity, relationship type, and residence status; additional questions were asked about weight, weight change, and weight control behaviors of the first three people listed. For example, the question "How would you describe the current body weight of ___?" provided response options of "underweight; normal weight; overweight," and "How would you describe the change in weight during the past year of ___?" provided response options of "weight did not change much; lost weight; gained weight; gained weight because of pregnancy." Participants were asked to report the weight control behaviors over the past year of each social contact – for example, if they ate low-calorie meals, ate small portions, or joined a commercial weight loss program.

When the researchers measured the participants' weight control behaviors and weight twelve months later they found some fascinating results: *Women and those in their social networks were alike in use of weight control strategies and weight change.* For example, women who reported ties to people who had lost weight were more likely to report that they themselves ate smaller portions and low-fat foods. The study reported similar information on a variety of other weight control behaviors, such as use of dietary strategies, exercise, meal replacements, and self-monitoring strategies. The researchers concluded that people who are connected to more individuals who engage in weight control behaviors may then emulate these behaviors through their greater exposure to information and modeling, as well as by adhering to a social norm within the social network. Box 3.1 highlights how the specific social network of friends and family can support or sabotage an individual's efforts to control their weight.

---

[11] Marquez, B., Norman, G., Fowler, J., Gans, K., & Marcus, B. (2018). Weight and weight control behaviors of Latinas and their social ties. *Health Psychology: Official Journal of the Division of Health Psychology, American Psychological Association* 37(4): 318–325. https://doi.org/10.1037/hea0000597

Box 3.1 The Influence of Close Social Networks: Support and Sabotage[12]

Close family and friends can more directly influence weight by saying and doing things that provide support or sabotage weight control efforts. In studies that have assessed people's perceptions of support and sabotage from their social networks, certain themes emerge. These include:

Positive: Offering to work on healthy habits together or encouraging healthy behaviors can be positive influence on how well an individual can stick to a weight loss program:

> *Well, my friend just joined a gym and she is working out and eating good. She asked me to join and walk together at work and eat more health[y].*
> *My daughter is especially supportive of healthy eating habits and encourages me to exercise.*

Negative: Sabotage from network members can take many forms, such as refusing to eat healthy together, spending time being inactive and not eating healthy together, and actively undermining efforts:

> *My family does not/will not eat healthy foods. It makes it very hard for me to watch what I eat.*
> *My friends ... are conscious of healthful eating and great cooks, but mostly sedentary, fond of sugar and alcohol, and talk about being active more than actually being so, including me!*
> *My boyfriend often brings home high-calorie and high-fat foods and tempts me with them. This is especially hard for me to resist when I have just gotten home from work and I am very tired and hungry.*

Another study of young women supports these statements. In this study, researchers found that perceived social support from family for healthy diets was associated with a lower BMI for participants, and a higher rate of sabotage of healthy diets and physical activity from friends was associated with a higher BMI of participants.

Romantic partners, especially those who live together, typically have daily contact and enact routines together (e.g., eat meals together), so weight loss occurs in an intricate, relational context that both partners shape. This

---

[12] Dailey, R. M. (2018). Exploring the role of the romantic relationship context in weight loss. *Journal of Social and Personal Relationships* 35(5): 679–701. https://doi.org/10.1177/0265407517693430. Theiss, J. A., Carpenter, A. M., & Leustek, J. (2016). Partner facilitation and partner interference in individuals' weight loss goals. *Qualitative Health Research* 26(10): 1318–1330. https://doi.org/10.1177/1049732315583980. Ball, K., & Crawford, D. (2006). An investigation of psychological, social and environmental correlates of obesity and weight gain in young women. *International Journal of Obesity (2005)* 30(8): 1240–1249. https://doi.org/10.1038/sj.ijo.0803267

interdependence is reflected in the health concordance between partners such as partners' diet and exercise[13] becoming more similar over time[14] and partners' BMIs being correlated.[15]

Social support, particularly from close relationship partners who share a home environment, can be highly beneficial in health behavior maintenance. However, a shared living environment can enable as well as hinder weight loss pursuits. Many studies that look at how cohabitating partners influence each other suggest that support from romantic partners in weight loss is generally helpful,[16] particularly when the partner co-participates in the weight loss program.[17] For example, one diary study found that on days when spouses provided support and encouragement about following their partner's recommended diet, their partners with type 2 diabetes were more

[13] Di Castelnuovo, A., Quacquaruccio, G., Donati, M. B., de Gaetano, G., & Iacoviello, L. (2009). Spousal concordance for major coronary risk factors: a systematic review and meta-analysis. *American Journal of Epidemiology* 169(1): 1–8. https://doi.org/10.1093/aje/kwn234. Meyler, D., Stimpson, J. P., & Peek, M. K. (2007). Health concordance within couples: a systematic review. *Social Science & Medicine (1982)* 64(11): 2297–2310. https://doi.org/10.1016/j.socscimed.2007.02.007

[14] Bove, C. F., Sobal, J., & Rauschenbach, B. S. (2003). Food choices among newly married couples: convergence, conflict, individualism, and projects. *Appetite* 40(1): 25–41. https://doi.org/10.1016/S 0195-6663(02)00147-2. Homish, G. G., & Leonard, K. E. (2008). Spousal influence on general health behaviors in a community sample. *American Journal of Health Behavior* 32(6): 754–763. htt ps://doi.org/10.5555/ajhb.2008.32.6.754. Falba, T. A., & Sindelar, J. L. (2008). Spousal concordance in health behaviour change. *Health Services Research* 43(1 Pt 1): 96–116. https://doi.org/10.1111/j.1475 -6773.2007.00754.x

[15] Pachucki, M. A., Jacques, P. F., & Christakis, N. A. (2011). Social network concordance in food choice among spouses, friends, and siblings. *American Journal of Public Health* 101(11): 2170–2177. https://doi.org/10.2105/AJPH.2011.300282

[16] Black, D. R., Gleser, L. J., & Kooyers, K. J. (1990). A meta-analytic evaluation of couples weight-loss programs. *Health Psychology* 9(3): 330–347. https://doi.org/10.1037/0278-6133.9.3.330. McLean, N., Griffin, S., Toney, K., & Hardeman, W. (2003). Family involvement in weight control, weight maintenance and weight-loss interventions: a systematic review of randomised trials. *International Journal of Obesity and Related Metabolic Disorders: Journal of the International Association for the Study of Obesity* 27(9): 987–1005. https://doi.org/10.1038/sj.ijo.0802383. Verheijden, M. W., Bakx, J. C., van Weel, C., Koelen, M. A., & van Staveren, W. A. (2005). Role of social support in lifestyle-focused weight management interventions. *European Journal of Clinical Nutrition* 59 (Suppl. 1): S179–S186. https://doi.org/10.1038/sj.ejcn.1602194

[17] Gorin, A., Phelan, S., Tate, D., et al. (2005). Involving support partners in obesity treatment. *Journal of Consulting and Clinical Psychology* 73(2): 341–343. https://doi.org/10.1037/0022-006X .73.2.341. Golan, R., Schwarzfuchs, D., Stampfer, M. J., Shai, I., & DIRECT Group (2010). Halo effect of a weight-loss trial on spouses: the DIRECT-Spouse study. *Public Health Nutrition* 13(4): 544–549. https://doi.org/10.1017/S1368980009991273. Kumanyika, S. K., Wadden, T. A., Shults, J., et al. (2009). Trial of family and friend support for weight loss in African American adults. *Archives of Internal Medicine* 169(19): 1795–1804. https://doi.org/10.1001/archinternmed.2009.337. Brownell, K. D., & Stunkard, A. J. (1981). Couples training, pharmacotherapy, and behavior therapy in the treatment of obesity. *Archives of General Psychiatry* 38(11): 1224–1229. https://doi .org/10.1001/archpsyc.1981.01780360040003. Dubbert, P. M., & Wilson, G. T. (1984). Goal-setting and spouse involvement in the treatment of obesity. *Behaviour Research and Therapy* 22(3): 227–242. https://doi.org/10.1016/0005-7967(84)90003-2

likely to adhere to their diet on the following day. But, on days when spouses exerted pressure or coercion (perhaps intended as support), partners were less likely to adhere to their diet on the following day.[18] Partners can also undermine weight loss efforts in other ways, such as tempting them with unhealthy foods, refusing to eat the same diet, interfering with their scheduled exercise, or making disparaging comments about their efforts.[19]

Box 3.2 Romantic Relationships and Weight Loss

In a study of how romantic relationship context plays a role in individuals' weight loss efforts, researchers interviewed people who were pursuing weight loss and who were living with their romantic partner. Those trying to lose weight were asked to indicate their subjective perspectives on their partner's support. Researchers analyzed the transcripts of their responses and several themes emerged: Participants overwhelmingly wanted a team effort and wanted their weight loss to be a joint effort or shared goal.

One participant noted:

"Well I would love it if we were more of a team" (F, 59).

Another expressed that working as a team made the process more enjoyable:

"Yeah, we're doing it together as a team. Yeah, we're talking about it – This is what we're gonna do, and we're gonna do it together" (M, 24).

Another participant commented that:

"I believe that is kind of the most gratifying thing – knowing that you and your partner are into doing something and don't have to convince them that they are already going to be on board with it. [We] kind of aligned our goals and wants in the same way, so it is fun to do it along with your partner" (F, 29).

Some participants also gave mixed reactions to the same type of message at different times. One participant described:

"He tries to help if he sees me eating something, 'Should you be eating that?' So it helps me to go, 'Oh yeah, you're right.' Sometimes I would get upset, and I'm like, 'Really, you get to eat it, why can't I?'" (F, 48).

---

[18] Stephens, M. A. P., Franks, M. M., Rook, K. S., et al. (2013). Spouses' attempts to regulate day-to-day dietary adherence among patients with type 2 diabetes. *Health Psychology* 32(10): 1029–1037. https://doi.org/10.1037/a0030018

[19] Henry, S. L., Rook, K. S., Stephens, M. A. P., & Franks, M. M. (2013). Spousal undermining of older diabetic patients' disease management. *Journal of Health Psychology* 18(12): 1550–1561. https://doi.org/10.1177/1359105312465913. Mackert, M., Stanforth, D., & Garcia, A. A. (2011). Undermining

These findings are consistent with weight loss interventions dating back to the 1980s that show that co-participation yielded the best results, and they parallel other research showing that individuals feel hindered in their weight loss progress when their partners resist healthy changes. Although assistance from friends, coworkers, or health care professionals can be helpful, romantic partners are in a unique position to offer a collaborative approach to weight loss given their shared household and routines. Simply accommodating dietary or schedule changes or offering logistical support could provide the needed spirit of unity.

The experience of weight stigma – a person's perceived social devaluation because of weight – has emerged as a key relational factor that affects weight loss and weight maintenance over time. This type of stigmatization is common in our society and is also a frequently neglected relational factor in obesity and weight loss treatment.[20] The stigmatization and stereotyping of body weight are well-known societal tropes, including assumptions that people with overweight and obesity are lazy, gluttonous, lacking in willpower and self-discipline, incompetent, unmotivated to improve their health, noncompliant with medical treatment, and thus personally to blame for their higher body weight.[21] These kinds of stigma and discrimination – from quiet expressions to overt inappropriate or derogatory comments – are experienced across many contexts, including work, health care, and interpersonal relationships such as with family members and friends.[22]

The paradox is that, although weight stigma can potentially increase individuals' *motivation and intention to lose weight,* it appears to simultaneously *decrease their capacity to do so* through healthy dieting and exercise. Instead, it can lead to an internalization of the stigma where people come to believe and repeat to themselves the societal messages about weight, triggering thoughts such as "My weight is a major way that I judge my

of nutrition and exercise decisions: experiencing negative social influence. *Public Health Nursing (Boston, Mass.)* 28(5): 402–410. https://doi.org/10.1111/j.1525-1446.2011.00940.x. Rydén, P. J., & Sydner, Y. M. (2011). Implementing and sustaining dietary change in the context of social relationships. *Scandinavian Journal of Caring Sciences* 25(3): 583–590. https://doi.org/10.1111/j.1471 -6712.2010.00867.x

[20] Puhl, R. M., Himmelstein, M. S., & Pearl, R. L. (2020). Weight stigma as a psychosocial contributor to obesity. *The American Psychologist* 75(2): 274–289. https://doi.org/10.1037 /amp0000538

[21] Puhl, R. M., & Heuer, C. A. (2009). The stigma of obesity: a review and update. *Obesity (Silver Spring, Md.)* 17(5): 941–964. https://doi.org/10.1038/oby.2008.636

[22] Phelan, S. M., Burgess, D. J., Yeazel, M. W., et al. (2015). Impact of weight bias and stigma on quality of care and outcomes for patients with obesity. *Obesity Reviews: An Official Journal of the International Association for the Study of Obesity* 16(4): 319–326. https://doi.org/10.1111/obr.12266

value as a person"[23] and "I feel anxious about being overweight because of what people might think of me." Shame or embarrassment may influence some people to attempt losing weight through unhealthy means (e.g., vomiting, fasting). A large national study of more than 6,000 US adults found that participants who experienced weight discrimination (as measured by self-report to questions such as: "You are called names or insulted" or "You are treated with less respect than other people are") were approximately 2.5 times more likely to become obese by a four-year follow-up weight and height measurement. Study participants who were obese at baseline were three times more likely to remain obese at follow-up than those who had not experienced such discrimination. This association between weight discrimination and obesity status in this study did not vary by age, sex, ethnicity, or education. Furthermore, weight stigma can lead to avoidance of places or experiences that could lead to further discrimination. For example, the more people report having experienced weight discrimination, the more they avoid exercising where weight stigma might occur, such as at exercise classes and gyms.[24] A major source of weight stigma stems from misperceptions about the individual's role in weight gain, and a major consequence is that it makes weight loss even more difficult.

Weight stigma contributes to weight gain in a cycle, as illustrated by Tomiyama's 2014 cyclic obesity/weight-based stigma model (Figure 3.1). Stigma is characterized as a stressor that elicits psychological (shame, stress responses), behavioral (increased eating), and biological (elevated stress hormones) responses, which in turn can contribute to weight gain and interfere with weight loss. As this cycle illustrates, even though behavioral and biological responses to stress are often discussed as completely separate processes, they are deeply intertwined.[25] In addition to weight gain, there are broader health implications of social devaluation. Psychologists have found that obese people that report a high frequency of experiencing weight discrimination also report declines in self-rated functional abilities and health over a ten-year period.[26]

[23] Durso, L. E., & Latner, J. D. (2008). Understanding self-directed stigma: development of the weight bias internalization scale. *Obesity* 16(S2): S80–S86. https://doi.org/10.1038/oby.2008.448

[24] Vartanian, L. R., & Shaprow, J. G. (2008). Effects of weight stigma on exercise motivation and behaviour: a preliminary investigation among college-aged females. *Journal of Health Psychology* 13 (1): 131–138. https://doi.org/10.1177/1359105307084318. Vartanian, L. R., & Novak, S. A. (2011). Internalized societal attitudes moderate the impact of weight stigma on avoidance of exercise. *Obesity* 19(4): 757–762. https://doi.org/10.1038/oby.2010.234

[25] Berkman, L. F., Kawachi, I., & Glymour, M. M. (2014). *Social Epidemiology* (p. 516). Oxford University Press.

[26] Schafer, M. H., & Ferraro, K. F. (2011). The stigma of obesity: does perceived weight discrimination affect identity and physical health? *Social Psychology Quarterly* 74(1): 76–97. https://doi.org/10.1177

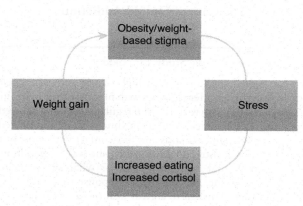

Figure 3.1 Tomiyama's cyclic obesity/weight-based stigma model.[27]

A clear conclusion from the research on relational effects on obesity is that dietary attitudes and behaviors (and resulting weight gain and loss) do not occur in isolation, but rather are part of a larger social environment, including close relationships and the family system. Support from one's network, community, or coaching relationships can be leveraged to improve weight loss. Despite the vast evidence of multiple relational influences on weight gain, individual factors continue to get a disproportionate amount of attention. One reason is that relational contributors are often more difficult to identify and address. Yet despite the difficulty, there is much value in doing so. It seems hard to imagine how behavioral strategies to increase Tomlinson's motivation for weight loss would make any lasting impact on his dietary habits without also addressing the relational forces that influence his complicated relationship with food. According to Robert Lustig, an obesity expert at UCSF, personal responsibility for weight as a sole factor is "Just another urban myth to be busted by real science."[28]

/0190272511398197. Sutin, A. R., & Terracciano, A. (2013). Perceived weight discrimination and obesity. *PLoS One* 8(7): e70048. https://doi.org/10.1371/journal.pone.0070048

[27] Tomiyama, A. J. (2014). Weight stigma is stressful: a review of evidence for the cyclic obesity/weight-based stigma model. *Appetite* 82: 8–15. https://doi.org/10.1016/j.appet .2014.06.108.

[28] Lustig, R. H. (2013). *Fat Chance: Beating the Odds Against Sugar, Processed Food, Obesity, and Disease.* Penguin.

The Case of Opioid Addiction

Case Study 3.1: Nikki[29]

Nikki, now 24, started smoking pot in high school and experimented with a few things early in college. Her struggles with heroin started in her junior year when she began a relationship with JP, who regularly used and showed her how to snort the drug. As she increasingly spent time with JP and moved into his apartment, she saw less of her friends and lost contact with most of them.

Her stepmother, who entered her life when she was 12, had long thought that Nikki needed mental health support for what she perceived to be unusually volatile behavior, particularly in response to any limit-setting by her dad or stepmother. This led to a great deal of stress for her stepmother, who felt that "you never knew what you'd get" from Nikki from day to day. But despite getting a DUI at nineteen and wrecking "multiple" cars, neither the mental health concerns nor obvious substance use was addressed. Nikki was "functional" and "fell under the radar." Her continued strong grades in college and maintenance of a full-time job were evidence enough to others that her stepmother was overreacting to substance use that "wasn't that big of a deal."

When she landed in the emergency room after a violent incident with JP, she admitted to her family that she had been using heroin along with other substances. She spent five days in a treatment for withdrawal and five weeks in rehabilitation. She was also diagnosed with bipolar disorder but has resisted taking medication or going to therapy to address her disorder. Her stepmother is hopeful that the worst is behind them and thinks that Nikki is staying away from heroin. However, she suspects that Nikki is "using other things that are tying her over."

A high percentage of people with opioid use disorder, like Nikki, also have other risk factors, most frequently co-occurring mental health disorders and trauma. Data from the 2016 *National Survey on Drug Use and Health* suggest that among adults who misused opioids in the prior year, 42.8 percent also had a mental illness and 15.6 percent had a serious mental illness.[30] A 2017 study published in the *Journal of the American Board of Family Medicine* found that 51 percent of recipients of opioid prescriptions for physical pain suffer from depression, anxiety, and other mental health

---

[29] Author interview, February 2021.
[30] National Institute of Health (NIH). (2019). Optimizing collaborative care for people with opioid use disorder and mental health conditions. NIH HEAL Initiative. https://heal.nih.gov/research/n ew-strategies/optimizing-care

conditions.[31] Ripple effects of addiction occur as well, so that if a close family member develops an addiction, other family members are also at risk for developing mental health issues. Some of the people getting these prescriptions (or getting opioids through other routes) then, are in fact treating the symptom – "psychic wounds" experienced as physical pain[32] that arise from depression or other mental health issues – rather than the root causes; that is, the sources of their pain. In such instances, the opioids are not just ineffective but potentially expose people to additional risks of addiction and overdose.

Unless these underlying social sources of pain are addressed, the prognosis for curbing opioid misuse is not hopeful. Other kinds of pain (emotional, spiritual), which is in many cases intertwined with physical pain, can be caused by many factors, including lack of economic stability, crumbling communities and family structures, and declining faith in religious and civic institutions that once bound people together. In their book *Deaths of Despair*,[33] economists Anne Case and Angus Deaton describe how, more than in previous decades, greater numbers of people now report experiencing pain; the increases have been especially sharp for White people without a bachelor's degree. This increase in reported pain aligns with increases in the proportion of Whites with less than a BA reporting "fair" or "poor" health. It may follow, then, that some of this pain might be the consequence of poor health overall. However, Case and Deaton emphasize that the data is murky on this point. For example, the shifting landscape of work and work-related injuries shows that the labor market is shifting *away* from occupations normally associated with physical pain. Moreover, reported pain tends to *increase* with joblessness. They theorize that these data suggest explanations for reported pain that are beyond only physical sources and therefore beyond the scope of health care as we typically conceive of it. Other research has found that in much of the United States the counties with the lowest levels of social capital have the highest overdose rates.[34] Low social capital is associated with hopelessness,

[31] Davis, M., Lewei A., Haiyin L., & Sites, B (2017). Prescription opioid use among adults with mental health disorders in the United States. *JABFM* 30 https://doi.org/10.3122/jabfm.2017.04.170112

[32] Lopez, G. (2018, September 25). Solving America's painkiller paradox. Vox. Retrieved from www.vox.com/science-and-health/2018/9/25/17327976/opioid-epidemic-painkiller-prescriptions.

[33] Case, A., & Deaton, A. (2020). *Deaths of Despair and the Future of Capitalism*. Princeton University Press.

[34] Zoorob, M. J., & Salemi, J. L. (2017). Bowling alone, dying together: the role of social capital in mitigating the drug overdose epidemic in the United States. *Drug and Alcohol Dependence* 173: 1–9. https://doi.org/10.1016/j.drugalcdep.2016.12.011

social isolation, and lack of opportunity, which can all contribute to starting, and continuing to use, opioids.

For many people, the social isolation and financial insecurity brought on by the COVID-19 pandemic contributed to their distress and risk for overdose. An analysis by the Commonwealth Fund found that shortly after the pandemic started, monthly overdose deaths spiked 50 percent, to more than 9,000 deaths in May.[35] Additional estimates from the Centers for Disease Control and Prevention suggested that deaths remained elevated for much of the rest of 2020 and the Commonwealth Fund researchers estimated the year's total overdose deaths could have exceeded 90,000 – up from 70,630 in 2019. *That would be the largest single-year percentage increase in the past two decades.*

The development of addiction is marked by physiological and relational changes that are crucially interrelated. During the early stages of use people may start using the drug impulsively and for recreational purposes. However, as addiction develops, drug use becomes increasingly compulsive. The progression of drug addiction then involves alterations in normal brain circuitry that result in long-lasting drug-induced neuroplastic changes.[36] As drug use escalates and transitions into compulsive drug use, people also typically become increasingly impaired in their ability to function socially; for example, high severity and duration of substance dependence is related to higher levels of loneliness. Progressive social exclusion and marginalization, impaired social interactions, and lack of access to resources dominate the lives of those addicted to opioids. Research has not clarified the causal direction or dynamics of the physiological and relational association. It may also be that those who use substances more intensively are also those who are more likely to have difficulty maintaining relationships or more likely to be stigmatized by society,[37] and ultimately become lonelier as a result of social isolation and stigma. Low social integration is a risk factor of heavy alcohol and drug use, and higher levels of social integration are associated with decreased relapse risk among drug users who seek

[35] Commonwealth Fund (2021). The spike in drug overdose deaths during the COVID-19 Pandemic and policy options to move forward. Retrieved from www.commonwealthfund.org/blog/2021/spike-drug-overdose-deaths-during-covid-19-pandemic-and-policy-options-move-forward

[36] Herman, M. A., & Roberto, M. (2015). The addicted brain: understanding the neurophysiological mechanisms of addictive disorders. *Frontiers in Integrative Neuroscience* 9: 18. https://doi.org/10.3389/fnint.2015.00018

[37] Ingram, I., Kelly, P., Deane, F., et al. (2020). Loneliness among people with substance use problems: a narrative systematic review. *Drug and Alcohol Review*. https://doi.org/10.1111/dar.13064

treatment.[38] In this way, opioid addiction can be considered an *adaptation* to difficult life circumstances, which clearly become even more difficult as the addiction progresses. Even if people have high social integration when they start using drugs, those who continue to use can often become socially excluded, which in turn promotes continued drug use. This results in further social marginalization and exclusion – factors that promote further drug use.

The interconnected ways in which our bodies respond to chemical and social rewards suggest relational approaches that can be incorporated into addiction treatment. Stress provokes relapse to drug seeking in humans and lab animals, but stressors typically used in animal models of addiction are discrete, experimenter-imposed events such as foot shocks.[39] By contrast, stressful relapses for drug users are typically social; they include, for example, conflicts in the workplace and with the family, lack of social support, and problems associated with low socioeconomic status. Positive social experiences can provide many of the healthy, nondrug reinforcers that successfully compete with drug rewards and that might also protect against the negative consequences of social stressors. When we have positive social experiences, the brain triggers the release of opioids in the body in response. These endogenous opioids are a critical part of the brain's reward system. In mice, the pinnacle of positive social experiences is social grooming behaviors. Humans, thankfully, have a wider range of positive social experiences that can trigger these responses, such as verbal support or physical interaction.

Thus, an intriguing possibility suggested by neuroplasticity researchers is that social integration, by restoring normal function of endogenous opioid systems, can decrease the need to activate these systems through substance use and subsequently can decrease drug use and relapse. Improving the social integration of substance users through opportunities for housing, jobs, and meaningful relationships is critically important to decrease use. Impaired decision-making, which is both a risk factor for and consequence of substance use, diminishes the ability to function socially, and impaired decision-making and social exclusion form the elements of a vicious cycle of their own.

---

[38] Havassy, B. E., Hall, S. M., & Wasserman, D. A. (1991). Social support and relapse: commonalities among alcoholics, opiate users, and cigarette smokers. *Addictive Behaviors* 16(5): 235–246. https://doi.org/10.1016/0306-4603(91)90016-B

[39] Heilig, M., Epstein, D. H., Nader, M. A., & Shaham, Y. (2016). Time to connect: bringing social context into addiction neuroscience. *Nature Reviews: Neuroscience* 17(9): 592–599. https://doi.org/10.1038/nrn.2016.67

Another critical relational component is that social networks may provide access to and encourage use of opioids. In a study examining non-medical prescription opioid (NMPO) use and related risk behaviors among young adults in a region with markedly high prevalence of NMPO use and overdose death, social networks played a pivotal role in access and norms surrounding use.[40] In this research, participants were asked about aspects of their drug use, and they reported high levels of access to prescription opioids through prescriptions originally provided to family and friends. Participants described multiple social contexts for access and use, such as parties and other social gatherings. These findings highlight that any effort to address the tragic spread of opioid addictions and overdoses must address the context in which risk behaviors arise.

The Case of Loneliness, Isolation, and Depression in Older Age

Social relationships influence, and are influenced by, health and wellbeing, particularly in later adulthood. Social isolation and loneliness have been identified as especially relevant to the physical and mental health of older adults because circumstances of aging, such as relationship losses, medical problems, and functional declines, are predisposing factors.[41] Yet despite widespread knowledge that social relationships are an essential component to healthy aging, social isolation, loneliness, and depression are on the rise among the elderly, with the COVID-19 pandemic only exacerbating risk. One recent study found that during the COVID-19 pandemic, closeness to the individuals in their network attenuated the relationship between loneliness and depression.[42] COVID-related social isolation led to increased depression and loneliness in older adults, but notably those who maintained connections with social and relational networks had significantly less depression.

Loneliness and social isolation are distinct but related experiences.[43] The subjective experience of loneliness occurs when there is a perceived

[40] Yedinak, J. L., Kinnard, E. N., Hadland, S. E., et al. (2016). Social context and perspectives of non-medical prescription opioid use among young adults in Rhode Island: a qualitative study. *American Journal on Addictions* 25(8): 659–665. https://doi.org/10.1111/ajad.12466

[41] Donovan, N. J., & Blazer, D. (2020). Social isolation and loneliness in older adults: review and commentary of a National Academies report. *American Journal of Geriatric Psychiatry* 28(12): 1233–1244. https://doi.org/10.1016/j.jagp.2020.08.005

[42] Krendl, A. C., & Perry, B. L. (2021). The impact of sheltering in place during the COVID-19 pandemic on older adults' social and mental well-being, *Journals of Gerontology: Series B* 76(2): e53–e58. https://doi.org/10.1093/geronb/gbaa110

[43] Cotterell, N., Buffel, T., & Phillipson, C. (2018). Preventing social isolation in older people. *Maturitas* 113: 80–84. https://doi.org/10.1016/j.maturitas.2018.04.014.

discrepancy between an individual's desired and achieved level of social interaction. The absence of supportive or fulfilling relationships can increase loneliness and it is generally experienced as painful, distressing, and unpleasant.[44] Social isolation is an objective measure,[45] characterized as an absence or limitation in the quantity of social interactions. Life transitions and disruptive life events such as retirement and bereavement can increase the risks of both social loneliness and social isolation.[46] People can feel lonely even when they have many social relationships (unhappy marriages, for example, are associated with feelings of loneliness) and, similarly, people can be alone for lengths of time and not feel lonely.

Social norms surrounding aging can contribute to the experience of loneliness, isolation, and depression. Ageism,[47] a term describing the stereotyping, prejudice, and discrimination against people on the basis of their age, can take a range of forms. Encountering ageist attitudes in one's neighborhood and community can lead to behavioral withdrawal and avoidance. Whereas more transient experiences of devaluation can motivate people to reconnect with others, experiences with ageism suggest more pervasive and chronic devaluation,[48] which tends to increase social disengagement.

Some evidence suggests that social isolation is an initial state that can precede loneliness, low perceived social support, and the onset of depression.[49] Aspects of both the quality of social relations (social support, the presence of confidants, higher satisfaction with one's relationships) and quantitative aspects (social integration, church attendance) seem to have important impacts on depression in late life.[50] A National Academy of Science and Engineering report on loneliness and social isolation in older adults reports evidence from longitudinal studies suggesting that loneliness and social isolation are antecedent risk factors for the development of depression or worsening late-life depression in older

[44] Peplau, L. A., & Perlman, D. (1982). Perspectives on loneliness. In L. A. Peplau & D. Perlman (Eds.), *Loneliness* (pp. 1–18). Wiley.
[45] Cotterell et al. Preventing social isolation in older people.
[46] World Health Organization. (2021). Social isolation and loneliness among older people. Advocacy Brief.
[47] World Health Organization (2021). Ageing: ageism. Retrieved from www.who.int/news-room/questions-and-answers/item/ageing-ageism
[48] Richman, L. S., & Leary, M. (2009). Reactions to discrimination, stigmatization, ostracism, and other forms of interpersonal rejection: a multi-motive model. *Psychological Review* 116: 365–383.
[49] Schwarzbach, M., Luppa, M., Forstmeier, S., König, H.-H., and Riedel-Heller, S.G. (2014). Social relations and depression in late life: a systematic review. *International Journal of Geriatric Psychiatry* 29: 1–21. https://doi.org/10.1002/gps.3971
[50] Law, R.W., & Sbarra, D. A. (2009). The effects of church attendance and marital status on the longitudinal trajectories of depressed mood among older adults. *Journal of Aging and Health* 21(6): 803–823. https://doi.org/10.1177/0898264309338300.

adults.[51] It highlights the results of a study of over 11,000 older US adults which found that lower frequency of in-person social contacts was related to higher rates of depression.[52] In addition to increasing the risk for psychiatric disorders such as depression and anxiety (and their consequences, such as suicide), social isolation was also associated with a decreased quality of life, overall physical and mental health, and self-reported satisfaction with life. Depression, especially minor depression, is thought to be under-recognized and under-diagnosed, but the prevalence rates are estimated to be at approximately 25 percent for older adults according to the latest estimates by the Kaiser Family Foundation.[53]

The myriad factors that make older adults more vulnerable to loneliness and social isolation can be understood in an ecological framework. At the individual level, personal characteristics such as being widowed or divorced, being aged seventy-five years or over, having limited financial resources, living alone, experiencing certain life course transitions, suffering from declining health, poor vision or hearing loss, losing the ability to drive, and being a caregiver are all factors. At the relationship level, infrequent contact with social relations and family conflict, disruption, or dysfunction can play a contributing role. At the community level, living in an area with limited opportunities for social participation, high gentrification and residential mobility, and inadequate access to services, amenities, and public transportation can increase vulnerability. At the societal level, structural factors can influence whether social participation is encouraged or inhibited, including experiencing discrimination and marginalization, lack of social cohesion, and social norms which discourage social activity.

In a study of older adults and the context in which they live in Minneapolis, researchers found that those in poor physical or mental health were more likely to report social isolation.[54] In interviews, many

[51] Steptoe, A., Shankar, A., Demakakos, P., & Wardle, J. (2013). Social isolation, loneliness, and all-cause mortality in older men and women. *Proceedings of the National Academy of Sciences* 110(15): 5797–5801.

[52] Shankar, A., Hamer, M., McMunn, A., & Steptoe, A. (2013). Social isolation and loneliness: relationships with cognitive function during 4 years of follow-up in the English Longitudinal Study of Ageing. *Psychosomatic Medicine* 75(2): 161–170. https://doi.org/10.1097/PSY.0b013e31827f09cd

[53] Koma, W., True, S., Fuglesten Biniek, J., et al. (2020). One in four older adults report anxiety or depression amid the COVID-19 pandemic. Retrieved from www.kff.org/medicare/issue-brief/one-in-four-older-adults-report-anxiety-or-depression-amid-the-covid-19-pandemic.

[54] Finlay, J. M., & Kobayashi, L. C. (2018). Social isolation and loneliness in later life: a parallel convergent mixed-methods case study of older adults and their residential contexts in the Minneapolis metropolitan area, USA. *Social Science & Medicine (1982)* 208: 25–33. https://doi.org/10.1016/j.socscimed.2018.05.010

respondents reported challenges with socialization due to their physical limitations:

> Before [the surgeries] I volunteered and was very active and social, but now . . .
> I had to quit a lot of them because I had a knee replacement and a hip
> replacement . . . I'm a little afraid to be on the ice, but yet I'm bored to tears
> staying home.
>   I do a little visiting every now and then, but other than that I'm
> a homebody. Like I said, most of the time I stay in the house because
> I can't walk long distances. I can't stand a long time, I definitely can't
> squat, or bend either forward or backward. It just keeps me at home
> a lot.

Other work has confirmed these reports, and found that other physical limitations, such as hearing loss, contribute to communication difficulties that can strain social interactions and increase the risk of social withdrawal and loneliness.[55]

But some of the feelings of being alone stem from winnowing social networks in older age, as one study participant in the Minneapolis study described:

> It's very, very hard to make friends in later life . . . I've gone to women's
> groups. I've extended myself. Maybe I come on too strong? But it doesn't
> seem [to be the case], because so many people have their children and now
> their grandchildren. They don't need friends.

And the fears that are sparked by this aloneness:

> It dawned on me one day that I could be laying here on the floor for a week,
> and nobody would even notice. That scared me a lot, you know?

Activities that bring meaning to life in later ages, such as serving or contributing to the community, can be difficult to access. These activities may even be discouraged by family or caregivers for concerns of physical safety.

Social science research shows that physical and social environments can play a significant role in the healthy aging of older adults. If these environments undergo rapid change, older adults may be adversely affected in ways that are beyond their individual control.

---

[55] Yorkston, K. M., Bourgeois, M. S., & Baylor, C. R. (2010). Communication and aging. *Physical Medicine and Rehabilitation Clinics of North America* 21(2): 309–319. https://doi.org/10.1016/j .pmr.2009.12.011

Case Study 3.2: The Rapid Change of Gentrification[56]

Gentrification refers to a process generally characterized by the redevelopment of neighborhoods to accommodate higher standards of living, often resulting in dramatic changes to how neighborhoods look. However, for long-time residents, the more important changes are the ones made to the social tapestry that had long held communities, families, and friends together.

Manish Kumar led a study that considered the impact of rapid change – gentrification – on a group of older adults living in affordable housing in Washington, DC. In interviews he conducted with residents, he found that they all generally viewed gentrification as beneficial to their neighborhood's physical environment. However, a common theme throughout the interviews with these older adults was their frustration and sadness over the loss of their social connections and the benefits they felt those social connections provided.

One sixty-two-year-old woman lamented, "It's a lot of prejudice [here]. It is. It's the people that has moved up and around the neighborhood. They don't really know me, or they come with the attitudes from where they came."

A sixty-eight-year-old man observed, "And then on the weekends we have the 18th St. corridor, which is a party scene. There's a lot of late night hoopin' and hollerin'. All kind of activities going on. So it's a little bit challenging, especially for old folks. I guess young people can get away with it."

Challenges posed by changes like these can further older adults' risk for social isolation, especially as the changes here are independent of individual characteristics or decisions.

Older adults are often not able to take advantage of technology that may serve as important sources of connection for other demographic groups. Technologies that are specifically designed to help older adults – including smart home sensors, robots, and handheld devices – can increase loneliness and social isolation if they are not easy and comfortable to use or if they serve as a substitute for human contact. In a trial study of older adults, frustrated users of digital assistants such as Amazon's Alexa cited difficulties using the voice-activation feature and low levels of perceived support for learning the technology.[57] Even videoconferencing, such as Zoom, which became ubiquitous during COVID-19, can present challenges to older adults without technological experience.

---

[56] Kumar, M., & Richman, L. (2020) Challenges and supports to aging in place in a gentrifying context. *Innovation in Aging* 4(Suppl. 1): 873. https://doi.org/10.1093/geroni/igaa057.3227

[57] Koon, L. M., McGlynn, S. A., Blocker, K. A., & Rogers, W. A. (2020). Perceptions of digital assistants from early adopters aged 55+. *Ergonomics in Design* 28(1): 16–23. doi: 10.1177/1064804619842501.

Case Study 3.3: Relationships and Technology for Older Adults[58]

Cindy, a seventy-seven-year-old widow living in an assisted-living center, tried to participate in a Zoom call for a celebratory dinner with her three children and their families, all of whom live in separate cities. She had been looking forward to the call for several days and when the time came she tried to connect, but reported, "I could hear everyone, but I couldn't get my video to work and they couldn't hear me." After about 30 minutes of troubleshooting with her children and grandchildren she ended up hanging up and said the experience left her feeling "very depressed," even days after the incident.

Social isolation and loneliness among the elderly was on the rise before COVID-19 social distancing, but became even more extreme as a result of limited social contact designed to reduce the risk of infection and to protect physical health. This confluence of risk mitigation for COVID-19 and isolation has significantly amplified the risk of loneliness and depression among older adults, and it could be especially severe among Black Americans, who are less likely to have home broadband services (66 percent) compared with non-Hispanic White adults (79 percent), limiting opportunities for communication.[59]

In a study of social isolation and loneliness among San Francisco Bay Area (noninstitutionalized) older adults during the COVID-19 shelter-in-place orders, researchers found more than half of participants reported worsened loneliness due to COVID, and this was associated with depression and anxiety.[60]

One respondent reported:

> I feel some sadness in knowing that both my age and the time this will take to stabilize might prevent me from ever traveling easily and freely again in my life. It is a reality that I have to accept.

Among those who reported limited social interaction, people reported major limitations due to limited access or ability to navigate technology:

> I really wish I could use the computer . . . It's time I learn a little technology. I'll be stuck at home; the world will pass me by. All my friends are on the Internet.

---

[58] Author interview, April 2021.

[59] Chatters, L. M., Taylor, H. O., & Taylor, R. J. (2020). Older Black Americans during COVID-19: race and age double jeopardy. *Health Education & Behavior* 47(6): 855–860.

[60] Kotwal, R. S., Montgomery, H. R., Kotwal, B. M., et al. (2011). Eliminating preventable death on the battlefield. *Archives of Surgery (Chicago, Ill.: 1960)* 146(12): 1350–1358. https://doi.org/10.1001/archsurg.2011.213

Other interviewees who were successful in navigating new technology reported more computer-mediated social interaction such as Zoom exercise and book clubs that would ordinarily meet in person.

For older adults, nonkin ties and new family forms can be important sources of support, particularly when physical limitations and health problems escalate. Demographic changes in patterns of family formation are projected to lead to fewer traditional sources of informal support and care, such as spouses, adult children, and siblings, and will instead rely more heavily on extended kin ties. Long-term committed relationships, regardless of their kin or legal marital status, can provide sustained support and care in later life.

Friends have been found to play a unique role in older adults' emotional wellbeing by increasing levels of positive experiences encountered in daily life. In a study of adults sixty-five and older who resided in the Greater Austin area of Texas, participants were asked to keep a daily diary of their social experiences.[61] In the daily diary they completed surveys every three hours for 5–6 days and they reported their encounters with social partners and rated the pleasantness of each encounter – for example, "How pleasant was this interaction for you?" with available ratings from 1 (unpleasant) to 5 (pleasant). They also indicated whether they discussed stressful issues during these encounters and rated positive or negative mood. The results showed that encounters with friends were more pleasant and were associated with fewer discussions about stressful experiences compared to encounters with romantic partners or family members throughout the day. Encounters with friends were also associated with better mood, though this link only held for encounters with friends who were not considered close.

Although the sources are varied, there are certain life events that create higher risks for isolation and loneliness. Losing a close relationship in later life is one such experience. Many older adults will experience the loss of one or more close relationships during the course of their lives, with ramifications for their health and, often, for the reorganization of their social lives over time. Compared with matched controls, widowed individuals experience more physical symptoms, more acute cardiac events, higher rates of disability and illness, more hospitalizations, and an increased risk of

[61] Ng, Y. T., Huo, M., Gleason, M. E., et al. (2020). Friendships in old age: daily encounters and emotional well-being. *Journals of Gerontology Series B* 76(3): 551–562. https://doi.org/10.1093/geronb/gbaa007

premature mortality.[62] These health differences are most pronounced within the first six months of the spouse's death and tend to decline thereafter, although some studies find the increased risk of mortality to persist even ten years after the spouse's death.[63] More needs to be learned about factors that facilitate or hinder older adults' efforts to reorganize their social lives successfully following the loss or disruption of different kinds of social ties.

Psychologists have distinguished between two different streams of research that are rarely considered together.[64] However, both are valuable to further an understanding of how social relationships function in later life. One perspective emphasizes the distinct strengths of older adults' social relationships that emerge from selective engagement with rewarding social network members and relationship regulation strategies aimed at avoiding conflicts or minimizing their impact. In other words: *we get better later in life at figuring out who to spend time with and who to try to avoid.* These strengths provide the basis for many older adults to experience high levels of satisfaction with their social relationships and to derive health-enhancing social support and companionship.

The second perspective emphasizes areas of health-compromising vulnerability in the social relationships of older adults that stem from conflicts and misunderstandings that recur over time and disrupt important close relationships. Some high-conflict relationships can be difficult for everyone (not just the elderly!) to avoid, such as children or neighbors. Conflictual relationships or criticism from family members has been found to be significantly related to higher prevalence of depression in older adults.[65] The winnowing of social networks through relocation and death is usually unavoidable as we age and can increase vulnerability to depression.

The two perspectives of strengths and vulnerabilities provide different, yet complementary, insights into the health-related implications of older adults'

[62] Moon, J. R., Kondo, N., Glymour, M. M., & Subramanian, S. V. (2011). Widowhood and mortality: a meta-analysis. *PLoS One* 6(8): e23465. https://doi.org/10.1371/journal.pone.0023465. Stroebe, M., Schut, H., & Stroebe, W. (2007). Health outcomes of bereavement. *Lancet (London, England)* 370(9603): 1960–1973. https://doi.org/10.1016/S0140-6736(07)61816-9
[63] Ytterstad, E., & Brenn, T. (2015). Mortality after the death of a spouse in Norway. *Epidemiology (Cambridge, Mass.)* 26(3): 289–294. https://doi.org/10.1097/EDE.0000000000000266
[64] Rook, K. S., & Charles, S. T. (2017). Close social ties and health in later life: strengths and vulnerabilities. *The American Psychologist* 72(6): 567–577. https://doi.org/10.1037/amp0000104
[65] Mechakra-Tahiri, S., Zunzunegui, M. V., Préville, M., & Dubé, M. (2009). Social relationships and depression among people 65 years and over living in rural and urban areas of Quebec. *International Journal of Geriatric Psychiatry* 24: 1226–1236. https://doi.org/10.1002/gps.2250

close relationships. One serves to highlight the satisfying and health-protective social networks that older adults proactively shape over the course of their lives, and the other calls attention to potential limitations of some older adults' close relationships and how these limitations may jeopardize health and wellbeing and may point to possible targets for interventions.

This framework for understanding strengths and vulnerabilities of social relationships in the elderly can help guide relational solutions to address loneliness and social isolation. Such solutions involve finding ways to prioritize engagement with emotionally close social ties that contribute to high relationship satisfaction, low rates of conflict, and access to health-sustaining support and companionship. These strategies can be developed in partnership with how health care is delivered to the elderly while others involve opportunities within communities for older adults to develop alternative support networks. Because the elderly often become physically separated from networks that they might be able to participate in, by moving to an assisted-living or nursing home or moving out of their home after the death of spouse to a new neighborhood distant from family, fostering ways to engage with new communities is essential.[66]

Conclusion

Relational factors are critical to understanding and mitigating obesity, opioid use disorder, and depression in the elderly. Individual factors, such as motivation and willpower, are central contributors to better health, but relational factors contribute to the development and main-tenance of these personal strengths. One theme that runs through the three health outcomes is the role that relational support plays in motiv-ating behavior, whether it be toward the goal of weight control, use of nonopioid pain relief, or activities that bring meaning to life in later ages. Regardless of one's specific purpose, it is difficult to pursue activities that are in service of those goals unilaterally and without any influence or connection with others. Having a sense of purposeful behavior also fosters the development of supportive relationships, because purposeful activity that takes our focus away from and out of ourselves promotes social engagement.

[66] Torres, S. (2019). Aging alone, gossiping together: older adults' talk as social glue. *Journals of Gerontology Series B* 74(8): 1474–1482. https://doi.org/10.1093/geronb/gby154. Weston, S. J., Lewis, N. A., & Hill, P. L. (2021). Building sense of purpose in older adulthood: examining the role of supportive relationships. *Journal of Positive Psychology* 16(3): 398–406. https://doi.org/10.1080/17439760.2020.1725607

In order to understand programs and treatments that *do* work for people, it is important to know how far these treatments are from current standard care for obesity, pain and opioid use disorder, and elder care. To help understand this disconnect between treatments that work and the current care pathways, Chapter 4 focuses on how these conditions are managed within the health care system.

Current Practices of Medical Intervention for Obesity, Opioids, and Social Isolation

---

Key Points

- Current treatment of obesity, opioid use disorder, and depression in older adults within the health care system are not sufficiently meeting patient needs.
- Focusing primarily on the individual patient misses the crucial relational contributions to these health issues.

This chapter examines how obesity, opioid use disorder, and depression in later life have been characterized over time by the public and medical professionals. It briefly summarizes the prevailing health care recommendations and practices, which are primarily centered around an individualized and biomedical perspective. It then discusses their limitations.

Medical Treatment of Overweight and Obesity: A Brief History

Americans' body weight has been on a steady rise over the last several decades. The growing trend was so steep and alarming that, in the late 1990s, obesity was deemed to be an epidemic. In 2013, the American Medical Association officially recognized obesity as a chronic disease.[1] This decision was heralded as a major step toward destigmatizing obesity and shifting perceptions away from viewing obesity as a failure of willpower and instead toward acknowledging it as a condition deserving medical attention. The shift to assigning the label of "disease" to obesity

---

[1] Kyle, T. K., Dhurandhar, E. J., & Allison, D. B. (2016). Regarding obesity as a disease: evolving policies and their implications. *Endocrinology and Metabolism Clinics of North America* 45(3): 511–520. https://doi.org/10.1016/j.ecl.2016.04.004

was also intended to prompt the investment of more resources for research, prevention, and treatment.

Regarding obesity as a disease has also led to some significant and unexpected downsides. By considering obesity through a medical lens, people (society, those with obesity, health care providers) came to view it as a disease that needed to be "treated" with medical intervention.[2] The primary focus then became, and continues to be, changing the dietary behavior of the individual, rather than on more relational and public policy prevention approaches. Chapter 3 described the numerous social and relational forces that shape our consumption patterns and weight status. Addressing weight in a medical setting mostly ignores these factors. And since the medicalized approach is so focused on the individual, it echoes prior views that suggested that individuals hold all the power to control their weight, and the new disease orientation has done little to diminish the stigma surrounding obesity.

Current Recommendations and Practices for Medical Treatment of Obesity

The US Preventative Task Force – a panel of national experts in prevention and evidence-based medicine – makes annual recommendations to policy-makers and health care providers on recommended clinical preventive services (e.g., screenings, counseling services, preventive medications).[3] In 2018, they published a statement summarizing the research on behavioral strategies to reduce obesity. Four aspects were determined to provide the most benefit to a primary care plan: a focus on problem-solving with the health care provider to identify barriers to weight loss; self-monitoring of weight; relapse prevention; and peer support.

Despite these recommendations – several of which seem potentially oriented toward relational solutions – obesity treatment in the primary care setting remains focused on individual lifestyle modifications of diet and exercise. Health providers vary in communication styles and recommendations for addressing weight loss with their patients, but generally the first line of treatment is to offer behavioral advice on how to lose weight. This approach is aligned with what social scientists suggest are the most effective strategies to encourage behavior change. Providers, for example,

---

[2] Lantz, P. M. (2018). The medicalization of population health: who will stay upstream? *The Milbank Quarterly* 97(1): 36–39. https://doi.org/10.1111/1468-0009.12363

[3] US Preventative Task Force (2018). Behavioral weight loss interventions to prevent obesity-related morbidity and mortality in adults US Preventive Services Task Force Recommendation Statement. *JAMA* 320(11): 1163–1171. https://doi.org/10.1001/jama.2018.13022

may encourage their patients to set Specific, Measurable, Achievable, Realistic, and Time-sensitive (SMART) goals for losing weight.[4] In following this guidance, a physician might suggest to her patient to set a goal of walking thirty minutes a day, three days a week, for two months, rather than a more general goal of becoming more active. Another SMART goal suggestion might be to replace soda with water every day for the next month, rather than attempting to achieve the more difficult goal of giving up all sugar. The expectation is that by setting these specific, "achievable" goals, people will be more able to succeed with weight loss.

Clinical guidance also suggests specific techniques for treating patients who are not immediately interested in or ready to commit to a weight loss plan. The advice is to "counsel him or her to avoid further weight gain and continue to treat other risk factors or health concerns." The assumption seems to be that the patient had not already considered avoiding further weight gain. The advice also implies that once this messaging comes from a medical professional, the appropriate behavior will logically follow.

A stepped-up medical approach for treating patients with obesity is to offer or refer them to intensive lifestyle interventions.[5] These programs usually include a thorough plan that uses behavior change strategies for at least six months to increase physical activity, reduce caloric intake, and undergo behavior therapy to improve lifestyle habits. These kinds of in-person programs are systematically lacking in underserved communities, however. Increasingly, these treatments are being implemented through community- and commercial-based programs, as well as delivered by telephone, Internet, and smartphone platforms, which expand the reach of treatment but produce smaller weight losses than in-person approaches.

Another medicalized approach to addressing obesity is medication or "anti-obesity drugs."[6] These are FDA-approved treatment options for people with an especially high BMI or who have other serious health issues, such as diabetes or hypertension. These medications are considered a second line of defense that supplement behavioral lifestyle approaches but are short of the extreme intervention of bariatric surgery.[7] A range of

[4] Mayo Clinic. (2020, August 25). How to set weight-loss goals that actually work. Retrieved from: www.mayoclinic.org/healthy-lifestyle/weight-loss/in-depth/weight-loss/art-20048224

[5] Webb, V. L., & Wadden, T. A. (2017). Intensive lifestyle intervention for obesity: principles, practices, and results. *Gastroenterology* 152(7): 1752–1764. https://doi.org/10.1053/j.gastro.2017.01.045

[6] Srivastava, G., & Apovian, C. M. (2018). Current pharmacotherapy for obesity. *Nature Reviews: Endocrinology* 14(1): 12–24. https://doi.org/10.1038/nrendo.2017.122

[7] National Institute of Diabetes and Digestive and Kidney Diseases (2020, September). Definition and facts of weight-loss surgery | NIDDK. Retrieved from: www.niddk.nih.gov/health-information/weight-management/bariatric-surgery/definition-facts.

these medications are widely available, and though some are safer and more effective than others, they are generally not considered a sound long-term strategy.

Gastric bypass and other weight loss surgeries – known collectively as bariatric surgery – involve surgically changing the digestive system to help promote weight loss. Bariatric surgery, which is most often performed in hospitals or specialty clinics, is a very expensive procedure (averaging approximately $25,000, depending on the type of surgery and location). The surgery is considered an effective treatment for weight loss, but is also invasive, usually irreversible, can have undesirable side effects, and is not appropriate for people who have other health complications that can make bariatric surgery high-risk.

Belief in medical solutions to obesity also fuels the drive to develop new technologies to promote weight loss. But this drive to bring new products to market has generated limited medical value while further stigmatizing obesity and legitimizing punitive solutions. One device that has appropriately received much public scorn is the DentalSlim Diet Control intraoral device (Figure 4.1), or what the popular press has referred to as "a medieval torture device."[8] This device is an updated version of jaw wiring (maxillomandibular fixation), which was used in the 1980s to restrict the ability to open one's mouth, thus forcing consumption of a liquid diet. With jaw wiring, forty-five- to sixty-five-pound weight loss within six months was

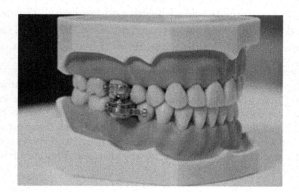

Figure 4.1 DentalSlim Diet Control intraoral device.

[8] Brunton, P. A., Ratnayake, J., Bodansky, H. J., et al. (2021). An intraoral device for weight loss: initial clinical findings. *British Dental Journal*. https://doi.org/10.1038/s41415-021-3081-1

common, but anxiety, acute psychiatric conditions, periodontal disease, and persistent limitations of jaw movement were eventually deemed as unacceptable side effects. More tellingly, as soon as the wires were removed, weight gain recurred and the majority of the patients rapidly returned to their pretreatment weight. The more modern DentalSlim Diet Control has a dentist fit magnets into the patient's upper and lower back teeth so wearers can only open their mouths 1/16 of an inch. Research participants, on average, lost about fourteen pounds after two weeks of wearing the device but suffered side effects of trouble pronouncing some words, occasional discomfort and embarrassment, and feelings that life in general was less satisfying. These patient reports have not dampened the developer's enthusiasm for the device. They continue to market it as an "economical and attractive alternative to surgical procedures," and describe the DentalSlim as a solution to poor patient adherence, which is "the main barrier to successful weight loss with dietary advice and restriction."

Limitations to a Medicalized Approach

Given the multiple strategies of a medical approach to obesity, it might seem perplexing that one approach, or some combination of them, is not more effective. There is nothing fundamentally misguided about weight loss interventions (with the exception of the DentalSlim) that aim to reduce the number of calories consumed. Even physicians in the pre-modern world attributed weight gain to an energy imbalance and recognized that obesity impeded good health and longevity. This awareness is documented in the writings of ancient Greece, Egypt, and India. Hippocrates, the fourth- to fifth-century BC Greek physician, wrote:

> All disease begins in the gut. Everything in excess is opposed by nature. If we could give every individual the right amount of nourishment and exercise, not too little and not too much, we would have found the safest way to health. Let food be thy medicine and medicine be thy food. It is very injurious to health to take in more food than the constitution will bear when, at the same time one uses no exercise to carry off this excess. The most famous doctors cure by changing the diet and lifestyle of their patient (Hippocratic Corpus).[9]

[9] Buchwald, H. (2018, July 20). A brief history of obesity: truths and illusions. Clinical Oncology. Retrieved from: www.clinicaloncology.com/Current-Practice/Article/07-18/A-Brief-History-of-Obesity-Truths-and-Illusions/51221?ses=ogst.

One problem with these strategies is that the obesity treatment guidelines are often not a good fit for how primary care is delivered. Some of these limitations become obvious if we examine common practice barriers. Even though health care providers are generally considered to be the most trusted source for obesity guidance, they are quite often not effective for several reasons. First of all, despite all the guidelines for physician practice, weight control is often not even addressed in a typical medical encounter. Unless a patient comes to their primary care doctor specifically to address their obesity (which is rare), and even when a patient's weight poses a risk for other health issues, clinicians generally focus on treating the associated health issues, such as diabetes, rather than the obesity itself. Researchers that conducted extensive interviews with physicians and nurses reported that providers have a general reluctance to prioritize weight with their patients.[10] Some felt discomfort in discussing weight issues; believed it was not their responsibility to address obesity (this was more true of physicians than of nurses); deemed that they lacked sufficient training and knowledge to treat obesity; and had a lack of confidence both in their patients' ability to institute changes and in the efficacy of available treatments. Providers also expressed stigmatized views of people with obesity.

Health care providers' perceptions of their patients impacts both the quality of care that they deliver and the outcomes that can be achieved.[11] Many health professionals, including those who specialize in the management of obesity, hold negative views toward people with excess weight. These negative views reflect the popular societal view that obesity is a consequence of a person's poor willpower.[12] Stigma can also reduce the quality of care for patients with obesity despite the best intentions of health care providers to provide high-quality care. Epidemiologist Sean Phelan and colleagues showed how stigmatizing attitudes of health care providers influence clinical perceptions, judgments, interpersonal behavior, and decision-making (Figure 4.2). Experiencing poor treatment from providers, or even expecting such treatment, causes patients to exhibit stress, avoid care, mistrust doctors, and resist treatment.

[10] Warr, W., Aveyard, P., Albury, C., et al. (2020). A systematic review and thematic synthesis of qualitative studies exploring GPs' and nurses' perspectives on discussing weight with patients with overweight and obesity in primary care. *Obesity Reviews*. https://onlinelibrary.wiley.com/doi/10.1111/obr.13151

[11] Puhl, R. M., & Heuer, C. A. (2009). The stigma of obesity: a review and update. *Obesity* 17(5): 941–964. https://doi.org/10.1038/oby.2008.636

[12] Phelan, S. M., Burgess, D. J., Yeazel, M. W., et al. (2015). Impact of weight bias and stigma on quality of care and outcomes for patients with obesity. *Obesity Reviews* 16(4): 319–326. https://doi.org/10.1111/obr.12266

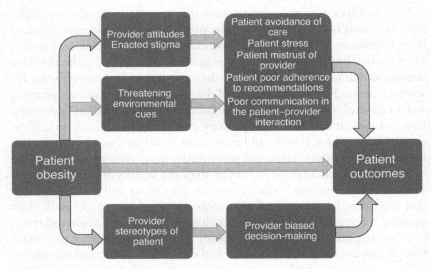

Figure 4.2 Conceptual model of the pathways by which health care providers' attitudes and behaviors about obese patients and patients' response to feeling stigmatized affect outcomes.[13] From Phelan et al.

Studies examining physician attitudes find that physicians rate individual-level factors – such as genetics, metabolism, depression, willpower, lack of knowledge, eating behavior, and exercise – as more important than environmental or relational factors in the development of obesity. These attitudes have remained constant despite (or perhaps due to) rising rates of obesity in the past two decades. The primacy that providers place on individual-level factors guides the strategies they favor in addressing weight management.

And even though health providers favor individual behavioral solutions to obesity, they tend to have low confidence in these strategies. Their views are shaped over time by common experiences with their patients. In my own interviews with primary care providers, a widely expressed sentiment was summarized by a family medicine doctor practicing in the western suburbs of Chicago, who stated simply: "Most people are really bad at losing and keeping off weight."[14] Primary care providers indicated that issues of obesity mostly arise in the context of improving the prognosis of other medical issues, such as when treating a patient for hypertension, diabetes, insulin resistance, or obstructive sleep apnea. Obesity raises the risk for several serious health

[13] Phelan et al., Impact of weight bias and stigma.   [14] Author interview, January 2021.

conditions, and it is these conditions that are addressed during the medical visit, rather than the obesity itself. The provider might describe how weight loss may mitigate the patient's primary problem and may point out the overall benefit of weight loss and its potential to eliminate the need for medications for their other conditions. Health care providers rarely directly observe relationship dynamics. For example, according to one physician, "I don't see much social interaction between patients and family. I may hear them talk about, for example, spousal comments about a need for weight loss, but I don't usually have firsthand access to those dynamics." They also do not typically ask about the relational factors that contribute to their patients' capacity to successfully achieve and maintain weight loss, despite the recognition that the majority of the hard work to enact behavior change takes place *outside* of the doctor's office, in homes, workplaces, and other settings. Consequently, the relational factors that contribute to the struggles with keeping weight off or that may contribute to successful long-term weight loss maintenance are most often not explored.

Even though the science underlying intensive behavioral weight loss strategies suggests that they should work, they simply do not reliably lead to sustained weight loss. Numerous studies have demonstrated that these interventions can be effective in getting people to lose weight. Evidence-based lifestyle modifications that rely on changes in diet and physical activity can produce weight loss of 5–10 percent, which translates into significant health benefits for people who have obesity.[15] However, it can be very challenging to maintain the weight loss, as a large percentage of people are not able to achieve and sustain clinically meaningful weight losses. The results show that most people regain at least one-third of their lost weight (even from these intensive programs) within a year without additional weight loss maintenance treatment.[16]

Conclusions about Treating Obesity

Treating obesity in the United States continues to rely on individual-level strategies, which include lifestyle modifications to diet and exercise, psychological services, medication, bariatric surgery, and medical devices. Health

---

[15] Wing, R. R., Lang, W., Wadden, T. A., et al. (2011). Benefits of modest weight loss in improving cardiovascular risk factors in overweight and obese individuals with type 2 diabetes. *Diabetes Care* 34 (7): 1481–1486. https://doi.org/10.2337/dc10-2415

[16] Wadden, T. A., Webb, V. L., Moran, C. H., & Bailer, B. A. (2012). Lifestyle modification for obesity: new developments in diet, physical activity, and behavior therapy. *Circulation* 125(9): 1157–1170. https://doi.org/10.1161/CIRCULATIONAHA.111.039453

care providers are often not equipped to address nonmedical influences. Information, advice, and support from health care providers can promote better dietary practices, but providers report many barriers to delivering obesity interventions, including lack of training, time, incentives, and confidence that patients will listen to and follow their advice. Without a better understanding of the relational contributions to obesity, both on the prevention and treatment ends, the current medical approaches to treatment will continue to be inadequate.

A Brief History of Pain and Opioid Use

The history of pain treatment and opioid prescribing in the United States shows a shift over time in attitudes. The Center for Disease Control and Prevention (CDC) traces the opioid crisis' trajectory and describes three discernable phases of prescribing and consumption trends.[17] The first phase began in the 1990s and consisted of a steady rise in opioid consumption, addiction, and rates of overdose. These developments were largely attributed to "supply-side" factors, namely aggressive marketing of prescription opioids, overprescribing by physicians, and lucrative opportunities across many sectors of chronic pain treatment. In an analysis of the origins and consequences of the opioid epidemic, drawing on recently unsealed documents from state litigation against Purdue Pharma, economists Carolina Arteaga and Victoria Barone argue that the aggressive marketing of prescription opioids was instrumental in increasing opioid use and overdose deaths.[18] They document efforts by Purdue Pharma to encourage physicians to prescribe opioids, spreading the message that millions of Americans were suffering from an epidemic of untreated pain and actively marketing OxyContin for its treatment. These targeted marketing practices have had long-term effects on opioid mortality, while also deteriorating socioeconomic conditions and worsening birth outcomes.

The second phase began in 2010. There was now an expanded pool of people with rising dependence and tolerance, many of whom transitioned from prescription opioids to more potent and cheaper alternatives, such as heroin. Overdose deaths tripled between 2010 and 2015.

The third phase extends from late 2013 through today and is marked by the emergence of extremely potent, illicitly manufactured fentanyl and its

[17] www.cdc.gov/opioids/basics/epidemic.html.
[18] Arteaga Cabrales, C., & Barone, V. (2021). The opioid epidemic: causes and consequences. Working Papers tecipa-698, University of Toronto, Department of Economics.

analogs, often as counterfeit pills and heroin. Between 2013 and 2016, fentanyl analog-related deaths spiked nationally and triggered the designation of the opioid epidemic as a national public health emergency. Although pharmaceutical companies, unscrupulous doctors, and others in the health care system were blamed for the first wave of opioid abuse, those entering drug treatment in this later phase were more likely to have started opioid use with heroin. The most recent opioid crisis dwarfs previous drug crises, both in terms of the number of people affected and the rate of increase in overdose deaths.

The opioid epidemic has had devastating effects on families and communities. A stark example of this is the dramatic increase in the number of children entering foster care due to parental addiction. In Ohio, children are entering foster care in record numbers, hitting 16,154 in 2018, an increase of 3,500 – or 28 percent – in five years. A Pew Research report finds that in Ohio nearly half of those taken into custody in 2020 had a parent using drugs, and case workers struggle to place children with relatives. By the time the children get to foster care, many of the adults in their extended family are also addicted to opiates.[19]

The history of the opioid epidemic and the current narratives about treating opioid use disorder has a racial component that deserves highlighting. This latest opioid epidemic has hit White communities particularly hard, and one reason is uneven prescription patterns of opioid analgesics for pain. Black people and Latinos in the United States have historically been less likely to receive opioid analgesics than White people, despite reporting similar pain complaints. Several large-scale studies of pain management in emergency room visits find that, compared to White patients, Black patients are significantly undertreated for pain, are less likely to have pain taken seriously, and are less likely to be prescribed opioids to treat it. The irony is that this bias may have saved some Black communities from being ravaged by opioid addiction. This trend is quickly changing though, as heroin and synthetic opioids, particularly fentanyl, are cheap and widely available. According to data from the National Center for Health Statistics, drug overdose death rates were higher in 2020 than in 2019 for all races and Hispanic-origin groups,

---

[19] Wiltz, T. (2016, October 7). Drug-addiction epidemic creates crisis in foster care. Pew Trusts. Retrieved from: http://pew.org/2dIqCEJ. Bush, B. (2018, December 21). Number of Ohio kids in foster care jumped by 3,500 in five years, largely due to opioid crisis. *The Columbus Dispatch*. Retrieved from: www.dispatch.com/news/20181220/number-of-ohio-kids-in-foster-care-jumped-by -3500-in-five-years-largely-due-to-opioid-crisis.

with non-Hispanic Black overdose death rates exceeding non-Hispanic White rates in 2020.[20]

Psychiatrist-anthropologist Helena Hansen and colleagues at UCLA have argued that current media-, community-, and policy-level responses to today's opioid epidemic have differed from responses to prior opiate epidemics by focusing on the dangers of the substances themselves,[21] rather than on the social conditions leading to widespread exposure to the substances.[22] Attention has focused on constricting access to opioid analgesics on the implicit assumption that addiction and overdose are being driven by powerful and uncontrollable forces – that is, the supply and pharmacological properties of the drug – rather than by the social conditions of demand. When attention is drawn toward social explanations, such as those offered in the "deaths of despair" argument advanced by Case and Deaton (see Chapter 3), calls for compassion are extended to the (until recently) mostly White communities affected by these drugs, rather than the judgments of moral deviance and criminalizing narratives that have historically described urban Latino and Black narcotic use.

Furthermore, the focus on this singular policy solution of curtailing overprescribing has fallen short of the intended effects. This can largely be attributed to the shift from prescription painkillers to heroin and other illicit opioids. Overall, supply-side prevention strategies are estimated to have minimal impact,[23] preventing only 3.0–5.3 percent of overdose deaths. According to addiction specialist Nabarun Dasgupta and colleagues "the strategy of restricting the supply of prescription opioids in response to historic overprescribing had little effect in reducing demand. *The source of the demand for these medicines* has not been adequately explored" (emphasis added).[24] The reality is that, even as we move away from "blaming the victim" for perceived moral failings and instead lay the blame on providers

[20] Hedegaard, H., Miniño, A. M., Spencer, M. R., & Warner, M. (2021). Drug overdose deaths in the United States, 1999–2020. NCHS Data Brief, no 428. https://dx.doi.org/10.15620/cdc:112340

[21] Alegria, M., Frank, R., Hansen, H., et al. (2021, January 21). Transforming mental health and addiction services | Health Affairs. Retrieved from: www.healthaffairs.org/doi/10.1377/hlthaff .2020.01472.

[22] Hansen, H. (2022). *Whiteout: How Racial Capitalism Changed the Color of Heroin in America.* University of California Press. Mendoza, S., Rivera, A. S., & Hansen, H. B. (2019). Re-racialization of addiction and the redistribution of blame in the white opioid epidemic. *Medical Anthropology Quarterly* 33(2): 242–262. https://doi.org/10.1111/maq.12449

[23] Pitt, A. L., Humphreys, K., & Brandeau M.L. (2018). Modeling health benefits and harms of public policy responses to the US opioid epidemic. *American Journal of Public Health* 108(10): 1394–1400.

[24] Dasgupta, N., Beletsky, L., & Ciccarone, D. (2018). Opioid crisis: no easy fix to its social and economic determinants. *American Journal of Public Health* 108(2): 182–186. https://doi.org/10.2105 /AJPH.2017.304187

or greedy profiteers, the ways in which pain and opioid use disorder are currently medically managed are still divorced from addressing the root causes.

Current Medical Management of Pain and Opioid Use Disorder

In the current medical model of addiction treatment, there is no pathway to address the sources of demand for opioids. The many causes of social pain – hopelessness, loss of community, low social capital – which are often intertwined with physical pain (see Chapter 3), are viewed as factors that are outside the scope of medical treatment. Undoubtedly, a lack of attention to nonmedical sources of social and physical pain in the treatment of addiction leads to inadequate care and rising trends in opioid use disorder. However, addressing the root causes of pain and opioid use is not the primary function of the health care system. Insurers, with an emphasis on profitability and cost-containment, have historically resisted paying for mental health care that could address these sources of pain. Addressing underlying issues that may ultimately result in cost savings by reducing the use of MRIs, surgeries, or other lucrative procedures to address pain may also run counter to revenue generation for health care systems.

The model for care and advocacy in the addiction and mental health field, usually referred to as "behavioral health," is to fund treatment programs and wait for "patients" with behavioral health conditions to show up for services. The focus is on treatment rather than prevention, and the result is "relentless unmet need." This model explains in part why the National Survey on Drug Use and Health estimates that in 2019 only 10 percent of people aged twelve or older who had a substance use disorder received needed treatment – estimates that are consistent with those of the four previous years.

For those who do manage to get into treatment, existing health care and treatment models are inadequate. They are rarely structured to facilitate treatment engagement support services that can lead to long-term remission of opioid use disorder.[25] As one addiction specialist notes, "We have lost the commonsense imperative to engage those who use opioids in

---

[25] McLellan, A. T., Lewis, D. C., O'Brien, C. P., & Kleber, H. D. (2000). Drug dependence, a chronic medical illness: implications for treatment, insurance, and outcomes evaluation. *JAMA* 284(13): 1689–1695. https://doi.org/10.1001/jama.284.13.1689. White, W., Kelly, J., & Roth, J. (2012). New addiction recovery support institutions: mobilizing support beyond professional addiction treatment and recovery mutual aid. *Journal of Groups in Addiction & Recovery* 7(2–4): 297–317.

comprehensive care, especially during periods when access to opioids may be fluctuating."[26]

Research shows that a combination of medication-assisted treatment (MAT) and behavioral therapy can successfully treat these opioid use disorders and help sustain recovery.[27] MAT is also used to prevent or reduce opioid overdose. The medications used in MAT (buprenorphine, methadone, and naltrexone), which are approved by the US Food and Drug Administration (FDA), work to facilitate withdrawal and block the brain reward circuitry of opioids. They operate to normalize brain chemistry, block the euphoric effects of opioids, relieve physiological cravings, and stabilize body functions without the negative and euphoric effects of the substance used. Although the most successful treatments combine MAT with counseling and behavioral therapies, many programs offer abstinence only, without any medication, or do offer MAT but without incorporating therapy or other relational strategies to address underlying causes of pain. In addition, the people who would supplement MAT with behavioral therapies – such as counselors, primary care physicians, peer groups, coaching, and mutual support groups – are insufficient and fragmented, creating barriers to recommended care.

Conclusions about Opioid Treatments

The individual, medicalized treatment of pain and addiction aligns with current payment and incentive structures for insurers and health care providers, but leaves vast unmet need. The underlying factors that play significant roles in creating and perpetuating pain – particularly mental health issues, social disconnection, a lack of purpose in life, and much more – are not adequately addressed. A medicalized approach to the unprecedented opioid epidemic, that is, treating primarily the physical addiction, falls short. Fragmented treatment and inconsistent access to evidence-based care have resulted in people suffering with addiction and not getting the treatment they need.

[26] Author interview, November 2020.
[27] Substance Abuse and Mental Health Services Administration (2021, October 13). Medication-assisted treatment (MAT). Retrieved from: www.samhsa.gov/medication-assisted-treatment. Substance Abuse and Mental Health Services Administration (2021, September 15). MAT medications, counseling, and related conditions. Retrieved from: www.samhsa.gov/medication-assisted-treatment/medications-counseling-related-conditions.

Social Isolation, Loneliness, and Depression in Older Adults

The proportion of older people relative to the rest of the population is rapidly increasing due to both a substantial increase in life expectancy, the aging Baby Boom generation, and a more recent trend of lower birth rates in the United States. Demographers estimate that by 2030, 20 percent of Americans will be age sixty-five or older. At the societal level, this population shift will continue to place great pressure on our fragile systems of health care, public health, and other supports for older adults. At the same time that demographic trends predict growing numbers of older people in the United States, social isolation has increased for this age group.[28] New cohorts of middle-aged adults, especially those aged 55–64 years old, have shown a major drop in social engagement with friends, family, volunteering, or work, presaging the likelihood of isolation in older age.

Social isolation increases the burden of illness and health care spending. According to a study of spending data by Medicare,[29] the federal insurance program that is the primary payer for health care services for virtually all Americans aged sixty-five and older, social isolation among older adults was associated with an estimated $6.7 billion in additional Medicare spending annually. The study found that after controlling for numerous baseline variables known to be associated with Medicare costs, the program spent an estimated $134 more monthly for each socially isolated older adult than it did for those who had more typical levels of social contact. This additional spending is comparable to what Medicare pays for certain chronic conditions, such as high blood pressure and arthritis. Moreover, health care costs for older adults with depression are approximately 50 percent higher than for older adults without depression.[30]

As described in Chapter 3, older adults are at increased risk for social isolation and loneliness because they are more likely to live alone, suffer the loss of family or friends, have a chronic illness, and experience sensory impairments. Data from numerous surveys show these high levels of isolation[31] and a 2018 study by the Kaiser Family Foundation found that more than one-fifth

[28] National Academy of Medicine (2016). *National Academy of Medicine: Annual Report 2016.* National Academy of Medicine. Retrieved from: https://nam.edu/wp-content/uploads/2017/05/2016-NAM-Annual-Report.pdf.

[29] AARP (2017, November). Medicare spends more on socially isolated older adults. Retrieved from: www.aarp.org/content/dam/aarp/ppi/2017/10/medicare-spends-more-on-socially-isolated-older-adults.pdf.

[30] SAMHSA (2011). Depression and older adults: key issues. Retrieved from: https://store.samhsa.gov/sites/default/files/d7/priv/sma11-4631-keyissues.pdf.

[31] Cudjoe, T. K. M., Roth, D. L., Szanton, S. L., et al. (2020). The epidemiology of social isolation: National Health and Aging Trends Study. *Journals of Gerontology Series B* 75(1): 107–113.

of adults in the United States say they "often or always feel lonely, feel that they lack companionship, feel left out, or feel isolated from others" and report that their loneliness has had a negative impact on various aspects of their lives.[32] As noted in previous chapters, the effect of deficient social networks and relationships on mortality is similar to that of other well-identified medical and behavioral risk factors such as smoking and hypertension.

However, experts have expressed concern that our nation is not prepared for the realities of an aging population: "Our health care system is unprepared to provide the medical and support services needed for previously unimagined numbers of sick older persons, and we are not investing in keeping people healthy into their highest ages."[33]

Missed Opportunities to Address Social Isolation in Elder Care

To date, a range of largely individual-level psychosocial interventions have been developed to reduce loneliness and social isolation in older adults.[34] With variable success, these interventions have attempted to improve social skills (e.g., through recreation activities), enhance social support (e.g., through mentoring and home visits), increase mediated social interaction (e.g., telephone outreach), and address maladaptive social cognition (e.g., psychological reframing). Many community-level approaches have been taken to improve social connections for individuals who are socially isolated or lonely, but opportunities to intervene may be most challenging for those who are at highest risk.[35] People who are in unstable housing situations, do not belong to any social or religious groups, do not have significant personal relationships, or otherwise do not have consistent interactions with others may never be identified in their own communities. Identifying and reaching those at highest risk are inherent limitations in community outreach efforts to combat social isolation.

However, as highlighted in a 2020 National Academy of Medicine report,[36] nearly all people fifty years of age or older interact with the health care system

[32] Kaiser Family Foundation and The Economist (2018). Survey on Loneliness and Social Isolation in the United States, the United Kingdom, and Japan (conducted April–June).

[33] Rowe, J. W., Berkman, L. Fried, L., et al. (2016). Preparing for better health and health care for an aging population: a vital direction for health and health care. NAM Perspectives Discussion Paper, National Academy of Medicine, Washington, DC. https://doi.org/10.31478/201609n

[34] Ong, A. D., Uchino, B. N., & Wethington, E. (2016). Loneliness and health in older adults: a mini-review and synthesis. *Gerontology* 62: 443–449. https://doi.org/10.1159/000441651

[35] SAMHSA, Depression and older adults.

[36] National Academies of Sciences, Engineering, and Medicine (2020). *Social Isolation and Loneliness in Older Adults: Opportunities for the Health Care System*. The National Academies Press. https://doi.org/10.17226/25663.

in some way. Frontline professionals working in primary care and social work are well placed to identify individuals who might be at risk. These points of contact, however, are often lost opportunities for health care providers to identify and act on social isolation. Currently, it is not standard practice for health care providers, particularly those without geriatric training, to screen for risk of isolation within the context of a health care visit. Despite the strong evidence for the significance of these relational factors, patients are rarely asked about them when they visit a health care provider. Some particular behaviors, such as smoking and drinking, that are risk factors for a range of diseases are routinely measured, but most others, such as if people have a network of people to provide necessary support for behavior change or whether people are at risk of isolation, have long been viewed as being outside the scope of medical practice and therefore are not measured when people visit their health care providers.

> The experiences of older people in our health care system are indicative of how current medical care is broken for all of us. We have created a society where we do everything possible to stay alive yet dread being old, a culture that discards people who don't fit the latest human "product specifications," and a health care system in which the work of medicine is often incompatible with both care and health.[37]

The needs of the elderly, beyond immediate physical concerns, are not adequately addressed by current medical care. Some of these deficiencies can be explained by health care providers receiving insufficient training to care for older people. Physicians, nurses, and care workers who have special training and expertise in caring for the elderly are in short supply, leading to a general deficiency in the recognition and management of common geriatric problems, such as risks for social isolation. In noninstitutional settings, as when elderly people live in their own homes, identifying isolation can be especially challenging.

Insurance benefits that could address some aspects of social isolation stemming from or exacerbated by social, economic, and environmental conditions are uneven. Most people over sixty-five remain insured under traditional fee-for-service Medicare, which incentivizes profit-generating services rather than flexibility and innovation in how to (directly or indirectly) address the needs of the elderly. Services that could especially benefit the elderly who are vulnerable to social isolation are not currently available for all older adults, such as expanded coverage from the Center for

---

[37] Aronson, L. (2019). *Elderhood.* Bloomsbury Publishing.

Medicaid and Medicare Services (CMS) via Medicare Advantage plans that offer home-delivered meals for people who have mobility limitations.

Most models of elder care in institutional settings, such as nursing homes, make significant efforts to promote socialization, but they often prioritize physical over emotional health. This is common practice, despite elder care residents' widespread preferences to increase socialization opportunities. Institutional settings provide the opportunity for social interaction and group activities, but fall short in staving off loneliness and depression.[38] As one nursing home resident described:

> I think that everybody gets it [depression] in a nursing home, because you're stuck in a place that you're not used to it. And it's a place that you really don't want to be stuck in [. . .] Some people in a place like this could feel a little bit forgotten, so to speak [. . .] Well, they provide bingo, which is a help. But there are some days when there are no activities like that. And it's lonesome. It gets very lonesome.

Conclusions about Isolation and Loneliness in Older Adults

Loneliness and social isolation in the elderly are rarely considered as components of mental or physical health and are most often left unidentified and unaddressed in current models of care. The relative lack of emphasis on prevention, a health care workforce with limited training in geriatric care, and inadequate care coordination all contribute to shortcomings in meeting needs. The health care system is currently unable to identify, prevent, and mitigate the adverse health effects of social isolation and loneliness in older adults.

Conclusions

Obesity, opioid use disorder, and loneliness, isolation, and depression in older adults have all shown upward trends in prevalence, suggesting that current health care strategies are not meeting needs. In general, current health care delivery practices are not attentive to underlying relational factors that promote and maintain these heath issues, and current medical interventions pay little heed to the broader social environment in which patients live. Each of the sections in this chapter illustrate that current

[38] Choi, N. G., Ransom, S., & Wyllie, R. J. (2008). Depression in older nursing home residents: the influence of nursing home environmental stressors, coping, and acceptance of group and individual therapy. *Aging & Mental Health* 12(5): 536–547. https://doi.org/10.1080/13607860802343001

practices define these conditions as a problem to be fixed with medical intervention, a response that has been characterized as "the medicalization of social problems."[39] What this means is that health care providers are asked to fix health issues that stem from factors that long pre-date the problems for which patients are seeking care. The disconnect between the inadequacy of the tools at providers' disposal and the perception that the solutions can be found in receiving more health care services drives up health care costs for everyone without improving population health or quality of life.

A misplaced priority on medical approaches misses opportunities for relational strategies that can improve treatment options. The relational causes for obesity, opioid use disorder, and risk factors for depression among the elderly can be more difficult to observe and require a different set of solutions than those required to improve physical symptoms presented at a medical visit. These are strategies that take into account an individual's network of peers, family, and community in approaches to prevention and treatment.

---

[39] Lantz, The medicalization of population health. Lantz, P. M. (2018). The medicalization of population health: who will stay upstream? The Milbank Quarterly 97(1): 36–39. https://doi.org/10.1111/1468-0009.12363

CHAPTER 5

Strategies for Relational Health Care

Key Points

- Relational health strategies build on existing communities of care in order to connect people with needed services.
- Health care delivery should measure and address social context when providing care, integrate social networks into treatment plans, and promote relationship building within the clinical encounter.
- For relational health to function correctly we must understand and reduce the stigma surrounding certain health problems.
- This chapter provides programmatic examples of how social connectedness can facilitate and support behavior change.

Box 5.1 Weight Management[1]

Anthony,[2] a middle-aged small business owner, has struggled to find the support he's needed for his weight loss goals. He said that he has avoided going to the doctor for as long as he can remember. He reports that his weight and height put him in the medical category of obese. The embarrassment and shame of being weighed and having to put on a gown that doesn't fully cover him was enough to cause him to avoid seeing a doctor. On the occasions when he couldn't avoid medical care, the doctor reminded him that if he lost weight, the symptoms of his autoimmune disease and back pain would be reduced, which left him feeling demoralized for days afterwards.

Almost ten years earlier he had gone through a difficult divorce and the possibility of dating again had been the impetus for him to lose over 120 pounds. By force of intense willpower, he drastically limited his calorie intake and cycled for forty-five minutes on a stationary bike while he watched

[1] Interview, May 2019.   [2] To retain anonymity, Anthony's real name is not being used.

Box 5.1 (cont.)

TV in the evenings. When he was successful in managing his weight, which to him meant being a "regular" size, he felt healthier and loved the compliments from his friends and customers.

Since then, he has gained and lost this weight twice and claims to have nearly a full wardrobe of clothes in six sizes. Although he says there are many reasons why he struggles with maintaining his weight loss, the main battles he reports are exhaustion and lack of motivation to sustain the effort it takes to keep the weight off. His work days are long and he often feels stressed. Despite his best intentions, thinking about carefully planning out his meals and monitoring his eating was often more than he felt able to handle.

Currently, he feels that he has the necessary support to maintain the good habit behavior, of which he knows he's capable. He's optimistic about his experience in a weight loss clinic that is part of the university hospital in the city where he lives. What he likes about the program, and what he says is different from his other weight management experiences, is that he has a team of people who are working with him and are in regular contact. He describes how a nutritionist monitors his weight and helps "create habits" for his meal planning. He's able to strategize with her about what to do when his motivation wanes. The majority of his care is delivered through messaging with his team. He has also enrolled in Overeaters Anonymous (OA), which meets weekly at a church close to his house. There, he is able to better understand his emotions around food and his body, which he thinks has helped him feel more motivated and reduced his feelings of shame. Through OA he was paired with a "buddy," who he talks with via phone two or three times a week and with whom he can plan his eating intentions and report to on his progress or setbacks.

Box 5.2 Pain and Substance Use Treatment[3]

Dr. Steven Prakken, a psychiatrist and former Director of Medical Pain Services at Duke University Health System, explains that addressing the social stressors that drive opioid misuse and finding the potential sources of support should be essential components to treatment for pain and addiction.

"The way I would look at social factors in our pain clinic is I do 60–90 minutes for an intake on 'pain psychology.' I don't ask 'do you do heroin' or 'drink.' I ask, 'What does heroin or <insert drug of choice> do to you? What's your relationship to it? Who's helping you with that? What does it look like in your life? What about the substance helps you?' What they are getting out of it

[3] Interview, December 2020.

Box 5.2 (cont.)

tells me what I need to help them with. Eighty percent of the misuse of opioids are for anxiety, pain, depression, etc. The information is not to define them, but find alternatives to fill that need. That nuance doesn't happen in most healthcare, which leaves people in poorly understood, poorly treated situations."

He continues, "To me, substance use disorders are decreases in social function and role capacity, when the world comes apart for you. It's not taking opioids, it's not even dying from heroin. This is a disease process and will always have a role in our society, but just treat it as best you can, don't make it pejorative."

As for what works: "The healthcare system has to give as much credence for substance use and mental health treatment as they do to the rest. If you get psych involved, it's going to reduce the cost because people are more taken care of. If you want to save money in the world, take care of the people who are hurting and in need."

Box 5.3 Social Connections for Older Adults[4]

Michelle Singleton, Director of Services at the Bernice Fonteneau Senior Wellness Center in Washington, DC, describes how the center offers participants a place for older adults to "come together to support each other in their wellness journey." Connections have developed through participation. She notes, "Since many participants live within walking distance, they've been able to connect with neighbors who didn't know they were neighbors. Once they make those connections, then they remain in contact." Participation in their offerings, which include fitness classes, nutrition, education and counseling support, health promotion, and social activities, are about 85–100 people per day (pre-COVID-19). The only requirements to participate are being at least sixty years old and a DC resident. Unique to many jurisdictions, all of the programs are free to the seniors.

People most often find out about the center from word of mouth – current participants tell their neighbors and friends, and people find them. They have also started to get physician referrals through patients who have been identified as at risk for social isolation and in need of fitness and nutrition support.

Ms. Singleton describes how people make use of their services in different ways. Some may come and stay for 20–30 minutes for exercise, a nutrition class, or congregant meal program, and some stay much of the day. During the COVID shutdown these connections have been invaluable sources of support,

---

[4] Interview, March 2021.

Box 5.3 (cont.)

comforting each other through the loss of personal family members and participants that have passed since the program closed a year ago, and helping with resources for home repairs and transportation. She notes various peer groups have formed from those connections, including a current events discussion group, a quilters club, and a nutrition class. The nutrition education classes and counseling are led by a registered dietician/nutritionist, the fitness classes and gym access (when in-person) are led by a certified fitness instructor, and the peer facilitators are seniors who have volunteered since the closure, and who send about twenty texts every week reminding their friends to come to the virtual classes.

One peer facilitator, Joycelyn, willingly accepted the request to lead what they call the "JAT Peer Group" (JAT being her initials). She is an energetic eighty-year-old participant who is very proud of her Guyanese heritage and demonstrates that through her love of Caribbean dance and music. She represented the center in the local "Ms. Senior DC Pageant," where she placed third. "Needless to say," reports Ms. Singleton, "dancing was her talent."

When asked to facilitate the group, Joycelyn took ownership of what she deemed her responsibility to get valuable information to her peers throughout the pandemic. She has worked with Ms. Singleton to coordinate speakers and activities, including virus and vaccine updates, and fire safety, since they are all at home more often. She makes certain that her group participants are reminded weekly to be in attendance. She also took the initiative to coordinate with the family of a participant who had a severe stroke to have her on the call just to listen and hear her friends from the center.

Perspectives on Relational Health

The three perspectives in Boxes 5.1–5.3 share features that are essential to any relational approach. Each contrasts the current *individualized* approach to health and wellness, which emphasizes willpower, self-reliance, and – primarily – medical solutions. A relational approach is one that instead seeks to understand how an individual's network of peers, family, and community can provide a positive force in achieving health goals. In Anthony's case, despite his motivation to improve his health by losing weight, he struggled to sustain the behaviors on his own. This led to a cycle of weight loss and gain that left him miserable. When he connected with the weight management clinic, which provided integrated care and a community-based support group, he gained a sense of confidence that he could carry through with long-term healthier habits. For substance use, pain management and mental health care need to be considered together in the treatment. When substance use is stigmatized and is addressed separately from the social conditions that surround it, then its treatment will be insufficient to address people's needs. For older adults, social isolation must be addressed at the community level – where older adults live. When community spaces enable people to share activities together and form friendships, they provide opportunities for older adults to socialize with their neighbors and create the networks necessary to reduce social isolation.

The focus of this chapter is to draw attention to the numerous methods by which relational health approaches can be used to improve upon how we address obesity, opioid use disorder, and elder care. These approaches rely on aspects of the "four socials" (Chapter 2) that, in addition to social support, also include social integration, social capital, and social norms.

This chapter highlights strategies that promote relational health and health care. These include:

1. Boosting community-level prevention efforts through place-based strategies within community resources;
2. Reducing the structural stigma associated with certain health issues and their treatment;
3. Social prescribing that identifies risk and protective network characteristics in the clinical encounter and bridges medical care and community resources; and
4. Positive relationship building between the provider and patient and among providers.

Relational strategies begin with community-level efforts to promote interaction and engagement with social resources. Recall the flowchart in Chapter 1 in which Berkman and colleagues stress the need to identify the "upstream" conditions that influence the development and structure of social networks. These include community and neighborhood factors that influence how social networks form, the kinds of resources and interactions they offer, the social norms they impose, and the myriad of ways they influence behavior.

Leveraging Relational Resources at the Community Level

A community is often defined as a group located in a particular geographic area. However, if broader definitions of communities are considered – ones that reflect shared responsibilities, struggles, or identities – then a wider range of relational resources become available. Such communities may include groups linked through culture, occupation, caretaking responsibilities, and more.

Using relational health concepts we can envision different communities transformed into avenues for support, integration, and positive social influence. The development, nurturing, and preservation of social networks creates opportunities to receive needed support. Importantly, both informal gatherings and formal support groups can encourage and support positive behavior change.

The Function of Public Spaces

Sociologists have examined how shared spaces can shape our interactions, finding that they can serve valuable functions of fostering contact, mutual support, and collaboration among friends and neighbors.[5] These spaces can include a range of possibilities so long as they have physical space where people can assemble, including public institutions, nonprofit organizations, and commercial establishments. These spaces play different roles in the local environment and support different kinds of ties. Some places, such as libraries, YMCAs, and schools, provide space for recurring interactions, often programmed, and tend to encourage more durable relationships. Others, such as playgrounds and street markets, tend to support looser connections that can also serve valuable functions.

A fascinating study of public spaces in New York showed just how valuable these public spaces can be for older adults who are vulnerable to social isolation. Research conducted by University of California, San Francisco medical sociologist Dr. Stacy Torres examined the socialization among older adults in some of these spaces.[6] Her primary data collection site was a café in close proximity to three residential complexes with affordable housing protections. These protections meant that many lower- to middle-income residents could remain in a rapidly gentrifying neighborhood and could "age in place."

Torres spent approximately 400 hours observing older adults in semi-private venues – for example, coffee shops and other retail spaces – and accompanied the observations with additional interviews. She paid particular attention to the function of gossip, and despite the bad reputation of gossip as a source of exclusion and hierarchy building, she found it also offers an important social connection for older adults living alone. Torres found that the time spent together to gossip in these spaces served as the

[5] Klinenberg, E. (2018). Worry less about crumbling roads, more about crumbling libraries. *The Atlantic*. Retrieved from: www.theatlantic.com/ideas/archive/2018/09/worry-less-about-crumbling-roads-more-about-crumbling-libraries.

[6] Torres, S. (2018). Aging alone, gossiping together: older adults' talk as social glue. *Journals of Gerontology: Series B*. https://doi.org/10.1093/geronb/gby154

"social glue" that reduced isolation and promoted wellbeing. In this way, she suggests that older adults can "age alone" by talking with and about others around them.

These and other studies illustrate the importance of creating public venues that support meaningful connections. They foster supplementary neighborhood-based networks that combat isolation. Public spaces that offer opportunities to interact and provide easy access to others, and that avoid membership fees or other financial responsibilities, are especially useful. These "easy access" spaces create opportunities for older adults who live alone to regularly interact with people, and these social network ties of familiar people have particular significance.

While those living in urban settings have greater opportunities to interact in a wider range of places closer to home, such as Dr. Torres' coffee shops, suburban or rural areas offer fewer accessible public spaces. Older adults living in these areas might instead turn to public libraries, schools, religious buildings, and community centers for social contact. These public facilities could advance public health if they are considered not only for the formal services they provide, but also as community resources for older adults to meet. In some communities, "hybrid third places" can provide services such as computer and yoga classes to older adults with no membership fee and can keep older adults engaged and connected to others.

Some promising programs that increase social connectedness focus on "place-based strategies" that provide long-term services and supports while also creating social networks within the community (the program in Washington, DC described at the beginning of the chapter is one such example).[7] Many communities also have "senior villages," which are neighborhood-based organizations supported by volunteers and which provide varied opportunities for older adults to socialize through group activities. This community design may be particularly effective in addressing loneliness since it can support activities based on shared interests, such as exercise groups, which research suggests are more effective than meeting for purely social reasons.

One such senior village in Bronzeville, a neighborhood in the south side of Chicago, has been in operation for the past twenty-seven years.[8] Its stated mission is to promote self-sufficiency for older adults through

[7] Jopling, K. (2020). *Promising Approaches Revisited: Effective Action on Loneliness in Later Life*. Campaign to End Loneliness. Retrieved from: www.campaigntoendloneliness.org/wp-content/upl oads/Promising_Approaches_Revisited_FULL_REPORT.pdf.
[8] The Village Chicago. (2021). Member stories. Retrieved from: https://thevillagechicago.org/mem ber-stories.

a network of support services, including a monthly support group for grandparents raising their grandchildren and relatives who are raising their dependents. These support groups encourage their members to "share their experiences, seek advice, or just listen." Meals are also provided to the members at each monthly meeting as a way to offer respite care and build community. Thoughtful interventions such as these can create the benefits that often come from high-social-capital communities. In this senior village, information on resources for the unmet needs of "community grandfamilies" are routinely incorporated into the regular support structure. In addition, expert guest speakers present on relevant topics that pertain to grandfamilies, such as legal guardianship, public benefits, and childhood development. Members report "a high-level of satisfaction with the support group, especially with regards to establishing an open forum for discussion and creating a supportive community of second-time parenting peers." This is all a product of constructing communities with an eye toward relational health.

Build Communication Infrastructure

Investments in public spaces can also facilitate useful information exchange between community members. Social groups and communities with a strong *communication infrastructure* are better equipped and prepared to cope with health stressors than communities that do not have this.

A strong communication infrastructure increases the availability of critical health information within communities and social groups. Investments in facilitating the growth of communication infrastructure can be particularly valuable for communities with low social capital. Access to health information tends to be socially patterned, where lower-resourced or less digitally connected communities have reduced access to important health information. This is most notably the case for members of immigrant groups, racial and ethnic minorities, and rural populations that may have both limited access to and less capacity to act on critical health information. These communities not only lack information, they also receive targeted advertising for processed foods and other unhealthy substances. One of the factors behind the steep rise in obesity rates has been the intensive marketing of high-calorie, nutrient-poor food in restaurants, on billboards, and other public spaces in lower-income communities.

Likewise, communities with relatively limited social capital or "community fragility" are particularly vulnerable to drug epidemics. In a study examining county-level data over fifteen years, researchers found a strong inverse association between a county's social capital and its drug overdose mortality rates.[9] Social capital may ameliorate overdose mortality through preventing the onset of drug-taking, aiding in the recovery of drug abusers, and reducing the fatality rate from overdoses. The researchers note that "social capital itself embodies connectedness between people, the antithesis of social isolation, and thus could interrupt the process of isolation and hopelessness that culminate in drug-taking." Information access and bridges to outside sources of support, "bridging capital," is particularly important for socioeconomically disadvantage communities who often need more support services than can be provided with their existing community networks.

Information networks can be created and maintained in communities through different mechanisms. Town hall meetings, for example, can engage community members in conversations about health problems, including those that require a coordinated response and active community participation. A strong communication infrastructure can also thrive on trusted intermediaries or knowledge brokers such as community-based leaders or local journalists. These intermediaries can enhance: awareness (drawing attention to relevant health information), accessibility (making health information more comprehensible to users), engagement (connecting health information to the unique problems and challenges faced by the community), linkage (connecting and coordinating information dissemination activities in the community), and mobilization (advocating for specific individual and collective actions based on available health information).[10]

Stigma Reduction

Stigma reduction, both at the societal level and in health care delivery, should be an explicit goal of relational health approaches and would be an expected byproduct. Feelings of shame, indignity, and embarrassment

[9] Zoorob, M. J., and Salemi, J. L. (2017). Bowling alone, dying together: the role of social capital in mitigating the drug overdose epidemic in the United States. *Drug and Alcohol Dependency* 173: 1–9. https://doi.org/10.1016/j.drugalcdep.2016.12.011

[10] Goulbourne, T., & Yanovitzky, I. (2021). The communication infrastructure as a social determinant of health: implications for health policymaking and practice. *Milbank Quarterly* 99(1): 24–40. https://doi.org/10.1111/1468-0009.12496. Wilkin, H. A. (2013). Exploring the potential of communication infrastructure theory for informing efforts to reduce health disparities. *Journal of Communication* 63(1): 181–200. McCormack, L., Sheridan, S., Lewis, M., et al. (2013). *Communication and Dissemination Strategies to Facilitate the Use of Health-Related Evidence.* Agency for Healthcare Research and Quality.

create barriers to behavior change and are counterproductive to achieving health goals.

Reducing Stigma in Obesity

Although it may be generally acknowledged that discrimination and stigma can be consequences of obesity, survey research has found that it is less common to perceive discrimination, racism, and other types of power imbalance as drivers of obesity. According to obesity researchers, "The public lacks a way of making sense of systemic imbalances in power and systemic forms of discrimination; as a result, people have a hard time thinking about how power inequalities might affect obesity rates."[11]

The pathways to reduce the stigma surrounding the health issues discussed in this book can take many forms. Educating family members and friends can suggest how to engage in supportive conversations about weight-related health. Addressing weight stigma within the context of a health care visit can improve some patient outcomes, including benefits for emotional wellbeing and health behaviors.[12] The *Strategies to Overcome and Prevent Obesity Alliance*,[13] an organization based at the George Washington University School of Public Health, offers recommendations to address gaps in provider training in obesity management. They encourage health care providers to discuss with their patients how weight loss can lead to a better quality of life, rather than merely focusing on cardiac and metabolic outcomes.

Patients are also less likely to feel stigmatized and more able to follow recommendations if providers engage in shared decision-making with their patients. This can involve assessing social context by using tools that allow patients to reflect drivers of gain and of loss, behavioral and eating practices that might be barriers to the lifestyle changes that are necessary for a successful outcome, and coping resources to manage stress.

[11] Puhl, R. M., & Heuer, C. A. (2010). Obesity stigma: important considerations for public health. *American Journal of Public Health* 100(6): 1019–1028. https://doi.org/10.2105/AJPH.2009.159491

[12] Carels, R. A., Young, K. M., Wott, C. B., et al. (2009). Weight bias and weight loss treatment outcomes in treatment-seeking adults. *Annals of Behavioral Medicine: A Publication of the Society of Behavioral Medicine* 37(3): 350–355. https://doi.org/10.1007/s12160-009-9109-4. Pearl, R. L., Hopkins, C. H., Berkowitz, R. I., & Wadden, T. A. (2018). Group cognitive-behavioral treatment for internalized weight stigma: a pilot study. *Eating and Weight Disorders* 23(3): 357–362. https://doi.org/10.1007/s40519-016-0336-y

[13] https://stop.publichealth.gwu.edu

Reducing Stigma in Opioid Use Disorder

For opioid use disorder, the shame and stigma of problematic drug use affects drug users, families, and communities, and prevents people from seeking the treatment they need. Currently, both the increased understanding of the science of addiction and the shifting demographics of the epidemic have contributed to reducing stigma and increasing compassion for people who suffer from addiction. For these reasons, the opportunities to increase treatment-seeking behaviors and adherence to treatment programs are more available than they have ever been.

Structural components of addiction treatment programs can also be modified to reduce stigma. Programs that integrate behavioral health care with the rest of care, rather than maintaining them as separate centers, can break down stigmatizing attitudes. Adequate funding for such programs needs to be made more available.

Adjusting frequently used language about substance use is also important for reducing stigma (Figure 5.1). Common terms such as "getting clean" can cast further shame, with the implication that people who

"ADDICTION-ARY" ADVICE

The Recovery Research Institute's glossary of addiction-related terms flags several entries with a "stigma alert" based on research that suggests they induce bias. A sampling:

ABUSER, ADDICT	DRUG
Use "person-first" language: Rather than call someone an addict, say he or she suffers from addiction or a substance-use disorder.	Use specific terms such as "medication" or "a non-medically used psychoactive substance" to avoid ambiguity.
CLEAN, DIRTY	**LAPSE, RELAPSE, SLIP**
Use proper medical terms for positive or negative test results for substance use.	Use morally neutral terms like "resumed" or experienced a "recurrence" of symptoms.

Figure 5.1 Suggestions for altering the language used when treating those with opioid use disorder.[14]

[14] Recovery Research Institute (2021). *Addictionary: Glossary of Substance Use Disorder Terminology.* Recovery Research Institute. Retrieved from: www.recoveryanswers.org/addiction-ary.

become dependent on opioids are tainted or dirty. The Recovery Research Institute at Harvard University suggests alterations in some common addiction-related terms that can further stigmatize people with opioid use disorder.

Instilling pride for people in recovery is more likely to lead to long-term treatment success. As one addiction specialist, Mary Bassett, notes, "It takes real courage to recover and we should celebrate it."[15] She argues that treatment programs should consider people with chronic drug use not as flawed human beings, but instead as people with a chronic illness that may sometimes relapse. "Just like those with diabetes or high blood pressure, people with substance dependency need compassionate and accepting responses to relapses."

Reducing Stigma in Loneliness, Social Isolation, and Depression

People who admit to feeling lonely can also elicit stigmatizing judgments from others. Although less research has been done to understand the stigma surrounding loneliness and isolation in older adults, some work suggests that when people are labeled as "lonely" they are perceived to be less likable, less attractive, and less preferred as a friend.[16] Although loneliness, isolation, and depression are distinct experiences, their overlap and growing prevalence suggest that normalizing these states is vital to providing effective solutions.

Beliefs that older adults have about aging, including the expectation of loneliness, disrespect, or disability, can also influence motivation for social engagement. Perceiving that loneliness and isolation are inevitable parts of aging can undermine interest in socializing and meeting new people. In the absence of new friendships or interactions with more peripheral social ties, older adults with negative expectations about aging may not maintain as much social support as they desire. Researchers examined how expectations of aging related to new friendship formation and social integration in a large sample of primarily older Black women in Baltimore, who were taking part in an intervention on volunteerism over the course of two years.[17] They

[15] Bassett, M. (2020, February 6). Addressing the opioid crisis: lessons learned from New York City. Retrieved from: www.hsph.harvard.edu/news/multimedia-article/addressing-the-opioid-crisis-lessons-learned-from-new-york-city.

[16] Mann, F., Bone, J., Lloyd-Evans, B., et al. (2017). A life less lonely: the state of the art in interventions to reduce loneliness in people with mental health problems. *Social Psychiatry and Psychiatric Epidemiology* 52. https://doi.org/10.1007/s00127-017-1392-y

[17] Menkin, J. A., Robles, T. F., Gruenewald, T. L., Tanner, E. K., & Seeman, T. E. (2017). Positive expectations regarding aging linked to more new friends in later life. *Journals of Gerontology Series B* 72(5): 771–781. https://doi.org/10.1093/geronb/gbv118

found that people who had higher expectations about aging at the start of the study (e.g., on a scale of 1 = definitely true to 4 = definitely false, higher average scores on items such as, "Being lonely is just something that happens when people get old") made more new friends two years earlier compared to those with more negative expectations. Other work has similarly found that expectations of loneliness in old age is associated with reports of being lonely over time.[18] This work suggests that interventions that address ageism and improve expectations about aging may also improve health in later life.

Social Prescribing: Identification of Network Characteristics and Connection to Support Opportunities

Health care providers and health care systems are increasingly recognizing that patients' social circumstances, including the quality of their social networks, should be considered as important contributors to their health. If clinical providers are aware of some of the relational factors that influence patients' health-related behaviors and health status itself, they then can develop more effective treatment plans. Health care providers can also strengthen routine procedures to assess and respond to relational needs through referrals or on-site social and legal services. Addressing these needs could ultimately save the health care system money and improve patients' quality of life. Researchers and physicians at the forefront of this effort advocated taking "psychosocial vital signs,"[19] just as blood pressure, height, and weight are measured at each health care visit. Identifying risk and protective network characteristics in the clinical encounter can then enable providers to bridge primary care and community resources.

The evidence is still emerging for how these psychosocial vital signs are best assessed and addressed in an active clinical setting. One such measure, the Protocol for Responding to and Assessing Patients' Assets, Risks, and Experiences (PRAPARE), is a standardized social risk assessment that patients complete when they arrive at their health care appointment.[20] Developed by the National Association of Community Health Centers (NACHC), this tool helps providers and health centers determine their

[18] Pikhartova, J., Bowling, A., & Victor, C. (2016). Is loneliness in later life a self-fulfilling prophecy? *Aging and Mental Health* 20(5): 543–549.

[19] Matthews, K. A., Adler, N. E., Forrest, C. B., & Stead, W. W. (2016). Collecting psychosocial "vital signs" in electronic health records: Why now? What are they? What's new for psychology? *The American Psychologist* 71(6): 497–504. https://doi.org/10.1037/a0040317

[20] National Association of Community Health Centers. (2021). PRAPARE (Protocol for Responding to and Assessing Patients' Assets, Risks, and Experiences). Retrieved from: www.nachc.org/research-and-data/prapare.

patient population's service needs. It is a twenty-two-item questionnaire that gathers information on personal characteristics like race and ethnicity, family, and home, and it asks questions about home life, financial security, social and emotional health, and isolation. The survey also asks questions about other social risks such as jail time, lack of transportation, and personal safety. Providers then incorporate these assessment data into the patient's medical record.

Numerous relational resources can be opportunities for support. Our existing social networks of close ties may include family members, friends, colleagues, and neighbors who can function as accountability partners. For health delivery, for example, a person's spouse, with whom they live and interact daily, can get involved in care coordination, such as helping to create home environments that support healthy behaviors. These support resources can assist programs for obesity, substance use, and social engagement by increasing awareness (a spouse who helps their partner avoid situations that could trigger substance use, or a neighborhood that devotes publicly accessible space for gathering and socializing), accountability (goal setting), and enjoyment.

The availability of social support from existing networks may be insufficient, or even detrimental, for some. Many people struggle with the skills that are necessary to maintain healthy and supportive relationships. In these cases, individuals need access to new sources of support, such as community programming or peer networks created through participation in recovery programs. When health promotion programs create opportunities for people to socially interact and develop these skills, there is more opportunity for success. Several services described in this chapter also incorporate social skills-building opportunities in their programs. Some examples of programs for obesity, opioid use disorder, and social isolation that leverage social resources outside of medical care include peer support programs and "place-based strategies" that work to create and foster social networks within the community and to provide assistance in securing long-term services and supports.

Relational Resources for Obesity

As noted throughout this book, the causes and origins of obesity are complex and multifaceted, and the most frequently prescribed strategies that rely on high-effort dietary and exercise habit changes have been unsuccessful in slowing the upward trend in Americans' weight. Relational health interventions can help adults lose or maintain weight by counteracting the forces, so many of which are out of our control, that promote unhealthy consumption patterns. These support structures are also valuable to buffer against social influences and interactions that undermine healthy eating efforts.

Weight loss efforts may particularly benefit from peer-based interventions that can offer support and establish norms. One such program, developed by Dr. Abby King, a population health scientist at Stanford, leverages the power of peers to promote physical activity and weight loss in what she refers to as "citizen scientists." These are novel interventions that explicitly target environmental factors and are designed to be enjoyable, convenient, adaptive, and supportive.

The programs are based on the commonsense premise that people are more likely to keep up an exercise routine if they find it convenient and enjoyable. Class or group instruction, which had their peak membership in the 1980s, are marketed as fun and social (think smiling spandex-clad fit people doing aerobics together), but can also be perceived as exclusive, embarrassing, and difficult to do for many people. Prior to COVID-19, many group-based physical activity programs had six-month dropout rates that can approach 50 percent. With the onset of COVID, membership rates are unlikely to make a resurgence to even these pre-pandemic levels.

In one study that harnessed peer support to promote physical activity, Dr. King and her collaborators trained Latino peer mentors to advise and support others in increasing their physical activity through regular communication.[21] Participants in this program successfully increased twelve-month walking levels in inactive older adults by an average of approximately 130 minutes per week over initial baseline levels. In other research, approaches that deliver in-person or peer-based support via a computer interface in community centers in low-income neighborhoods increased weekly walking and twelve-month weight loss (approx. five pounds) and lowered resting blood pressure levels among inactive Latino adults.

Online social networking services also have the potential to create supportive environments to combat obesity, but the parameters of these groups matter. When these groups lack a professional moderator who can flag inaccuracies, there is the potential for misinformation to spread. Challenges also arise in maintaining long-term participation in these groups.

[21] King, A. C., Bickmore, T. W., Campero, M. I., Pruitt, L. A., & Yin, J. L. (2013). Employing virtual advisors in preventive care for underserved communities: results from the COMPASS Study. *Journal of Health Communication* 18(12): 1449–1464. https://doi.org/10.1080/10810730.2013.798374. King, A. C., Campero, M. I., Sheats, J. L., et al. (2020). Effects of counseling by peer human advisors vs. computers to increase walking in underserved populations: the COMPASS randomized clinical trial. *JAMA Internal Medicine* 180(11): 1481–1490. https://doi.org/10.1001/jamainternmed.2020.4143

Successful obesity prevention programs can also benefit from incorporating long-term support opportunities into their models. These will necessarily be ongoing support efforts that are beyond the confines of a doctor's office and will rely on modalities that foster social support.

Relational Resources for Opioid Use Disorder

The Substance Abuse and Mental Health Services Administration (SAMHSA), an agency within the US Department of Health and Human Services (HHS), has the mission "to reduce the impact of substance abuse and mental illness on America's communities." SAMHSA emphasizes the role of relationships and social networks as crucial elements of recovery:

> The process of recovery is supported through relationships and social networks. This often involves family members who become the champions of their loved one's recovery. Families of people in recovery may experience adversities that lead to increased family stress, guilt, shame, anger, fear, anxiety, loss, grief, and isolation. The concept of resilience in recovery is also vital for family members who need access to intentional supports that promote their health and well-being. The support of peers and friends is also crucial in engaging and supporting individuals in recovery.[22]

Research shows that relationships and social networks are an essential part of successful opioid use treatment. Although treatment is often discussed in terms of dualities (e.g., support groups/psychosocial treatment vs. medications), the strongest evidence points to combining network support (behavioral therapy, self-help groups, peer support) with medications (buprenorphine, methadone, naltrexone) as playing essential roles in opioid addiction treatment.[23]

Examples of programs that have aligned these two modalities of network support and medication for addiction treatment have shown promising success. National mutual support groups such as Self-Management and Recovery Training (SMART Recovery) back the use of medication as part of the recovery process. Furthermore, community-based programs that seek to combine the strengths of peer support with evidence-based medication

---

[22] King et al., Employing virtual advisors in preventive care for underserved communities. King et al., Effects of counseling by peer human advisors vs. computers.

[23] Wen, H., Druss, B. G., & Saloner, B. (2020). Self-help groups and medication use in opioid addiction treatment: a national analysis. *Health Affairs* 39(5): 740–746. https://doi.org/10.1377/hlt haff.2019.01021

treatment are important shifts toward reducing stigma of medication treatment and improving treatment retention.[24]

The relatively recent and growing practice of training/certifying and employing peers to work in supervised treatment teams can improve a variety of recovery outcomes for both mental health conditions and substance use disorders (SUDs). Peer supports are a way to bridge the gap between detoxification and longer-term SUD treatment by helping patients enter residential programs or engage with recovery programs in the community.[25]

Self-help groups, which are organized as mutual aid programs with mentorship and support provided by peers in recovery, can serve as sources of ongoing support from outside of existing networks. Some, like the Narcotics Anonymous twelve-step program or SMART Recovery, have been recognized by the American Society of Addiction Medicine as psychosocial treatment and are considered a useful addition to specialty addiction treatment provided by health care professionals. Online networks and hybrid "telehealth," which combines in-person visits with treatment that is provided by video or phone, are additional examples of longer-term support opportunities. Other interventions that aim to positively impact treatment outcomes through targeting the improvement of social connections may be less successful due to attrition and perceived irrelevance to recovery.[26]

Many health care institutions have begun to implement peer recovery support services (PRSS), a relatively new model of relational care, to help people with SUD and co-occurring psychological disorders. PRSS are peer-driven mentoring, education, and support services that are delivered by people who themselves experienced SUD and recovery. PRSS programs support engagement with substance treatment programs and transitions between inpatient and outpatient programs.[27] They also build social capital by connecting people with community-based recovery support services and mutual-help organizations.

[24] Krawczyk, N., Negron, T., Nieto, M., Agus, D., & Fingerhood, M. I. (2018). Overcoming medication stigma in peer recovery: a new paradigm. *Substance Abuse* 39(4): 404–409. https://doi .org/10.1080/08897077.2018.1439798

[25] Eddie, D., Hoffman, L., Vilsaint, C., et al. (2019). Lived experience in new models of care for substance use disorder: a systematic review of peer recovery support services and recovery coaching. *Frontiers in Psychology* 10: 1052. https://doi.org/10.3389/fpsyg.2019.01052

[26] Ingram, I., Kelly, P. J., Haslam, C., et al. (2020). Reducing loneliness among people with substance use disorders: feasibility of "groups for belonging." *Drug and Alcohol Review* 39: 495–504. https://doi .org/10.1111/dar.13121

[27] White, B. (2009). Peer-based addiction recovery support: history, theory, practice, and scientific evaluation. *Counselor* 10(5): 54–59.

A large area of SUD peer-service growth over the past decade has been in the uptake of peer recovery coaches. Recovery coaches are peers trained to provide informational, emotional, social, and practical support services to people with SUDs through recovery community centers, clinical settings, and other organizations.

PRSS roles emphasize that long-term recovery relies on the continuity of support from personal, familial, and community resources. Regardless of the nature of their role, peers have the ability to help people outside the confines of traditional clinical practice and fill critical care gaps for SUD. These services can be delivered in a variety of settings and with a range of service roles, including paid and volunteer recovery support specialists. Findings to date tentatively validate the potential of peer supports across a number of substance use treatment settings.[28] Evidence reveals positive results on measures including reduced substance use and relapse rates, improved relationships with treatment providers and social supports, increased treatment retention, and greater treatment satisfaction. Peer-led interventions for substance use seem to be effective even when contact with peers is limited. Researchers found significant reductions in substance use after six months from just a single-session peer-led intervention at a hospital-based walk-in clinic.[29] PRSS represent a promising method to deliver relational health care, but additional evaluation work is needed to identify which peer roles are most helpful in different clinical, treatment, and recovery support contexts.

For low-income Medicaid recipients, Medicaid Home Health models of coordinated care are a necessary advance in providing social support for opioid use disorder. The model integrates opioid agonist treatment with health care and social services. The Affordable Care Act (ACA) included several provisions designed to improve care coordination in state Medicaid programs for those with chronic conditions, including opioid use disorder. The program works through states being provided with enhanced federal matching funds for up to eight quarters to support Health Home programs that integrate primary and mental/behavioral health care and address social

---

[28] Valentine, P. (2011). Peer-based recovery support services within a recovery community organization: the CCAR experience. In J. F. Kelly & W. L. White (Eds.), *Addiction Recovery Management: Theory, Research and Practice* (pp. 259–279). Humana Press. https://doi.org/10.1007/978-1-60327-960-4_14. White, W. L. (2010). Nonclinical addiction recovery support services: history, rationale, models, potentials, and pitfalls. *Alcoholism Treatment Quarterly* 28(3): 256–272. https://doi.org/10.1080/07347324.2010.488527

[29] Bernstein, J., Bernstein, E., Tassiopoulos, K., et al. (2005). Brief motivational intervention at a clinic visit reduces cocaine and heroin use. *Drug and Alcohol Dependence* 77(1): 49–59. https://doi.org/10.1016/j.drugalcdep.2004.07.006

needs. In an analysis of three states – Maryland, Rhode Island, and Vermont – researchers found that these models identify needs, coordinate care, and reduce associated stigma.[30]

Community resources that can be valuable sources of support can also come from disease-specific national organizations. The National Alliance on Mental Illness (NAMI) is one such group.[31] This organization offers support groups for people with mental health conditions, as well as their families and friends. These support groups meet weekly and develop a community of people who share a common condition. NAMI is also actively involved in drawing attention to and advocating for change in stigmatizing portrayals of mental illness in the media. Disease-specific organizations like NAMI can play a crucial role in gathering resources, motivating behavior, advocating on behalf of members, and conducting campaigns to improve patient-centered care. Such organizations can also increase awareness and reduce misinformation. Disease-specific affinity groups may also form organically as communities within which people can share their experiences. Social networking platforms, particularly those that have some professional monitoring to protect against misinformation, can give people the tools they need to interact with others who share their diagnosis, gain access to new expertise and information, ask questions of members of their network, share updates about their health status, and receive emotional support.

Relational Resources for Elder Care

The identification of risk and protective network characteristics is particularly important for the care of older adults. Housebound older adults are known to be at greater risk of loneliness, social isolation, and health and social care problems when compared with the general population.[32] For older adults who are homebound, have no family, or do not belong to community or faith groups, a medical appointment or home health visit

---

[30] Clemans-Cope, L., Wishner, J. B., Allen, E. H., et al. (2017). Experiences of three states implementing the Medicaid health home model to address opioid use disorder: case studies in Maryland, Rhode Island, and Vermont. *Journal of Substance Abuse Treatment* 83: 27–35. https://doi.org/10.1016/j.jsat.2017.10.001

[31] www.nami.org/Home

[32] Qiu, W. Q., Dean, M., Liu, T., et al. (2010). Physical and mental health of homebound older adults: an overlooked population. *Journal of the American Geriatrics Society* 58(12): 2423–2428. https://doi.org/10.1111/j.1532-5415.2010.03161.x. Wenger, G. C., & Burholt, V. (2004). Changes in levels of social isolation and loneliness among older people in a rural area: a twenty–year longitudinal study. *Canadian Journal on Aging* 23(2): 115–127. https://doi.org/10.1353/cja.2004.0028

may be one of the few social interactions they have. These interactions with health care providers are a good point of entry to identify risks of social isolation and then connect them with opportunities for social connection. A 2020 report issued by the National Academies of Sciences, Engineering, and Medicine identifies the health care system as an underused partner in preventing, identifying, and mitigating social isolation in this group.[33] Primary care may be well positioned to identify and address limitations in relational health such as social isolation and connect people to needed resources. A wide range of relational-based interventions have been applied among older adults to address loneliness and social isolation, and some strategies can improve social connectedness as a way of enhancing the wellbeing of older adults. More work needs to be done on the characteristics of people who benefit the most (and least) from these interventions and to determine how to tailor interventions appropriately. For example, variability in the effects of social support may be attributable to differences in a person's initial risk status, social skills, or network relationships.[34] In addition, interventions that simply increase social networks and social engagement are not sufficient to decrease loneliness without concomitant feelings of support and satisfaction with those connections.[35]

The implementation of relational strategies to address loneliness and isolation in older adults is met with several challenges. Currently, the lack of consistency in strategies to identify lonely and socially isolated older adults has the potential to lead to a mismatch between the content of an intervention and participant needs.[36] Underscreening for these issues is more due to structural barriers, such as limited time in clinical visits, than a lack of measurement tools. Although both health care professionals and participants report the need for long-lasting interventions to create meaningful social networks, there is a lack of durable interventions at the present time.

If social isolation and loneliness needs are identified through a risk assessment, the tasks that health care providers are already performing – discharge

[33] National Academies of Sciences, Engineering, and Medicine. (2020). *Social Isolation and Loneliness in Older Adults: Opportunities for the Health Care System*. National Academies Press. https://doi.org /10.17226/25663

[34] Cohen, S., Underwood, L. G., & Gottlieb, B. H. (Eds.). (2000). *Social Support Measurement and Intervention: A Guide for Health and Social Scientists* (pp. xi, 345). Oxford University Press. https:// doi.org/10.1093/med:psych/9780195126709.001.0001

[35] Czaja, S., Moxley, J., & Rogers, W., (2021). Social support, isolation, loneliness, and health among older adults in the PRISM randomized controlled trial. *Frontiers in Psychology*. https://doi.org/10 .3389/fpsyg.2021.728658

[36] Galvez-Hernandez, P., González-de Paz, L., & Muntaner, C. (2022). Primary care-based interventions addressing social isolation and loneliness in older people: a scoping review. *BMJ Open* 12: e057729. https://doi.org/10.1136/bmjopen-2021-057729

planning, case management, and transitional care planning – can then be modified to directly address these needs. Once identified, patients at risk can be referred either to peer support groups or can be connected with social services that provide regular contact with providers of care services. Strategies are still needed to bridge silos between primary care and community resources. Primary care liaisons, employed by the Agency on Aging in the Seattle area, were offered as a way to integrate care and services by linking primary care with community-based programs that promote engagement and support. A feasibility study of this liaison model found increases in the referrals of primary care patients to community resources and increased capacity to connect patients, their families, and caregivers to these resources.[37]

In a program based in central Texas and New Hampshire, researchers collaborated with existing services for homebound seniors (home-delivered meals program, home health care) to deliver an intervention called *behavioral activation*, which is designed to improve social connectedness.[38] In both states, investigators developed meaningful research partnerships with regional aging-service providers that identified low social connectedness as a prevalent problem for the clients they served. Behavioral activation works by promoting meaningful life activities that align with personal values to decrease isolating behaviors. Lay coaches worked with participants to identify and schedule values-based, rewarding social engagement and activities and to use strategies to reduce and problem-solve barriers to social connectedness. Participants review their daily activity patterns and then choose activity goals, work on specific implementation plans, and review their areas for improvement over the course of five sessions.

This intervention shows encouraging findings. As compared to a group of seniors who received five sessions of friendly teleconference visiting, which is how social service agencies typically address isolation, the behavioral activation group of seniors had greater increases in social interaction and social satisfaction, and a decrease in loneliness, depression, and disability. This approach may be especially suited for improving social connectedness among homebound older adults, who often have limited opportunities for social engagement and were especially receptive to an

---

[37] Boll, A. M., Ensey, M. R., Bennett, K. A., et al. (2021). A feasibility study of primary care liaisons: linking older adults to community resources, *American Journal of Preventive Medicine* 61(6): e305–e312. https://doi.org/10.1016/j.amepre.2021.05.034

[38] Choi, N. G., Pepin, R., Marti, C. N., Stevens, C. J., & Bruce, M. L. (2020). Improving social connectedness for homebound older adults: randomized controlled trial of tele-delivered behavioral activation versus tele-delivered friendly visits. *American Journal of Geriatric Psychiatry* 28(7): 698–708. https://doi.org/10.1016/j.jagp.2020.02.008

active program that developed specific coping skills. Given the challenges of broadband access and cost, the feasibility of tele-delivery for underserved population groups will vary significantly. Future studies need to be conducted in partnership with community-based aging-service agencies to examine the scalability and sustainability of this approach.

During the COVID-19 pandemic, when videoconferencing capacity increased, short-term video or telephone-delivered support emerged as an effective short-term intervention for homebound older adults who experience social isolation, loneliness, or dissatisfaction with social support. The successful implementation of relational strategies such as these for older adults presents its own set of challenges and there continues to be a need to evaluate what contributes to successful programs and to expand the work that is being done in this area.

As part of a statewide loneliness intervention for the elderly, New York State's Office for the Aging in 2018 launched a pilot project that distributed *Joy for All* robots to sixty state residents and then tracked them over time to determine whether the robots reduced loneliness.[39] To date, more than 20,000 people have received *Joy for All* pets from state aging departments in twenty-one states.

Caseworkers, particular ones in more rural counties, reported liking the robots: delivering services to clients with robots was much easier than typical services that address loneliness and isolation. Prior to the robots, the caseworker would apply for grant funding for clients to attend a social program, which many did not attend because of trouble getting to the community center. The caseworker would also try to connect clients with caregivers in the community, but since Medicare does not cover long-term caregiving there was a shortage of available caregivers, making this option also out of reach for many clients. But large-scale evaluations have not yet been conducted to determine whether the robot pets were in fact effective. Although anecdotal reports are positive, the data are far from definitive. Regardless, the question of whether the robot pets actually work may be secondary to the perception that they offer a solution – perhaps imperfect and rife with ethical concerns – to what many who work with the elderly see as an intractable crisis of upward trends in social isolation. Importantly, these are trends that will only become a greater concern as the proportion of elderly in the population grows. Robot pets are just one of many

[39] Engelhart, K. (2021, May 24). What robots can – and can't – do for the old and lonely. *The New Yorker*. Retrieved from: www.newyorker.com/magazine/2021/05/31/what-robots-can-and-cant-do-for-the-old-and-lonely.

examples of such specialized technology. The so-called "silver market" or "loneliness economy" is huge and has been built around products to address loneliness and isolation in the elderly. In April 2018, the *Joy for All* leadership team left Hasbro and founded *Ageless Innovation*, which provides a range of products designed to address loneliness.[40]

Caution is warranted in turning to technology for solutions to loneliness and social isolation. Sherry Turkle, a sociologist and psychologist at MIT, has spent much of her career examining the relationships between people and technology. She warns that there is a psychological risk in the robotics movement and that robots designed to interact with humans on an emotional level "suggests a fantasy in which we cheapen the notion of companionship to a baseline of 'interacting with something.' We reduce relationships and come to see this reduction as the norm."[41]

Relationship Building between the Provider and Patient, and among Providers

The relationships *within* medical care delivery can improve the quality of care that is received and the willingness of patients to follow through on medical recommendations. Relationships between providers and patients and relationships among providers – the two that have the strongest evidence base – are also essential components of relational health.

The word "presence" for health care providers refers to a purposeful practice of awareness, focus, and attention, with the intent to understand and connect with patients.[42] Dr. Abraham Vergese, a physician at Stanford University, coined this term and advocates for its wide use in doctor–patient interactions. He suggests that when doctors practice presence, the gathering of nuanced, personal data (e.g., what is important to a patient and how a patient's symptoms affect their life, goals, and preferences for treatment) can cultivate respect and trust between patients and physicians and reduce miscommunication. Medical anthropology uses the term "idioms of distress" to refer to the ways that people make sense of, express, and then work to alleviate stressful feelings. This discipline recommends that, "Listening to the stories of somatized stress can provide clues to non-medical solutions that

[40] Ageless Innovation (n.d.). About. Retrieved from: https://agelessinnovation.com/about.
[41] Turkle, S. (2012). *Alone Together: Why We Expect More from Technology and Less from Each Other.* Basic Books.
[42] Verghese, A. (2016). The importance of being. *Health Affairs (Project Hope)* 35(10): 1924–1927. https://doi.org/10.1377/hlthaff.2016.0837

could prevent – or at least acknowledge – the underlying causes of the physical stresses individuals are experiencing."[43]

In an article in the *Journal of the American Medical Association*, a team of clinicians and researchers at Stanford reviewed the literature and interviewed providers, patients, and nonproviders to examine what "presence" means to these different groups. Based on this research, the team published recommendations for practices that have the potential to foster physician presence, meaningful connections with patients, and improve the experience of clinicians and patients.[44]

The researchers came up with five recommended "Presence 5 Practices" that all focus on ways in which providers can foster better relationships with their patients. These are:

1. Prepare with intention (take a moment to prepare and focus before greeting a patient).
2. Listen intently and completely (sit down, lean forward, avoid interruptions).
3. Agree on what matters most (find out what the patient cares about and incorporate these priorities into the visit agenda).
4. Connect with the patient's story (consider life circumstances that influence the patient's health; acknowledge positive efforts; celebrate successes).
5. Explore emotional cues (notice, name, and validate the patient's emotions).

These Presence 5 Practices enable the provider and patient to build trust and partnership with each other. They also provide the opportunity for patients to communicate about aspects of their social networks that are relevant for care, such as whether they have the needed support to follow through with health recommendations. The advantage of these practices is that they are relatively easy to adopt and disseminate – which could result in a greater population-level effect over time.

Importantly, though, these recommendations do not fully address the broader pressures that threaten the ability of the physician to practice presence. As described in Chapter 2, there are many obstacles to connection and relationship building in patient–physician encounters, including time

---

[43] Manderson, L., Cartwright, E., & Hardon, A. (2016). The Routledge Handbook of medical anthropology. Routledge.

[44] Zulman, D. M., Haverfield, M. C., Shaw, J. G., et al. (2020). Practices to foster physician presence and connection with patients in the clinical encounter. *JAMA* 323(1): 70–81. https://doi.org/10.1001/jama.2019.19003

pressures and competing priorities. Given the potential for relationship building to lead to better outcomes, there is more need than ever for cultural and structural changes within organizations to prioritize meaningful interactions.

Researchers who focus on the cost and quality of health care have begun to examine how the interconnectedness of individual physicians, hospitals, and medical groups influence patient care.[45] These studies have found that physicians, patients, and systems that exist within informal networks provide higher-quality care than less-networked physician practices. They do so by sharing information about patients, norms about quality practice, and current best practices. This work is in the early stages, but suggest possibilities for ways in which relationships within medical care delivery can improve the quality of care.

Conclusions

The innovative toolbox of relational health approaches described in this chapter can provide a path forward from relying solely on the individual to change their behavior to instead applying a wider selection of relational interventions. A truism of intervention work is that, when possible, it is more beneficial to develop interventions that can be embedded into ongoing practice and existing systems than to create ones that are resource-intensive and cannot be maintained in the long term.[46] To that end, the focus of this chapter has been on highlighting strategies that can be effectively integrated into practice and have been shown to provide sustained benefits. Programs and interventions that foster relational health can occur at the level of the family, group, or neighborhood, and often require collaboration with education, public health, housing, or other organizations to foster community building and improve health.[47] The essential features of relational health are put into practice through interventions aimed at increasing the social components of treatment for obesity and opioid use and incorporating the necessary socialization for elder care. Expanding weight and substance use

[45] O'Brien, E., et al. (2021). Pilot proposal, "Physician networks and cardiovascular outcomes in the Southeastern United States."

[46] World Health Organization. (2021). Obesity and overweight. Retrieved from: www.who.int/newsroom/fact-sheets/detail/obesity-and-overweight.

[47] Healthy People 2030. (2020). Social cohesion. Retrieved from: https://health.gov/healthypeople/objectives-and-data/social-determinants-health/literature-summaries/social-cohesion.

management approaches to include consideration of stigma could also help strengthen the impact of intervention efforts.[48]

Some of the featured programs are community-based and exist outside of the medical encounter. These include place-based strategies and communication infrastructures that facilitate high levels of social integration in communities and groups by connecting members to one another and to the collective problems they face. Other interventions are within the context of an interaction with a health care provider and emphasize modeling patient care as collaborative, with an emphasis on patient education and family support. Promising avenues for incorporating relational health into practices of health care delivery can be found across different contexts. A benefit to health care providers assessing relational factors is that, by doing so, they can connect patients to resources as part of their provision of care.

Unfortunately, despite the encouraging outcomes that have resulted from relational health approaches, many of these strategies and interventions have not received sufficient resources. In some cases this omission can largely be attributed to their novelty, and in many other cases the programs are firmly established but their results have not been broadly disseminated. In still other cases, where health policy is primarily focused on individual-level priorities, these relational approaches are neither accessible to nor discussed with the patient. As a result, population-level improvements continue to stagnate. Moreover, many of the interventions described lean heavily on volunteers, low-paid community health workers, and unstable funding that is often patched together from small grants, gifts, and donations. In order to grow and maintain these programs, more stable funding is critical.[49] Chapter 6 focuses on suggestions for key policy priorities to better align funding, research, and the delivery of care with a relational health approach.

---

[48] Puhl, R. M., Himmelstein, M. S., & Pearl, R. L. (2020). Weight stigma as a psychosocial contributor to obesity. *The American Psychologist* 75(2): 274–289. https://doi.org/10.1037/amp0000538

[49] National Academies of Sciences, Engineering, and Medicine, Social Isolation and Loneliness in Older Adults.

CHAPTER 6

Relational Health Policy Priorities

Key Points

- Relational health policy priorities focus on building opportunities for network support.
- The policy priorities include strengthening social and health care integration, mobilizing community resources, and enhancing workforce skills training.

Chapter 5 focused on strategies for putting relational health into action and highlighted some interventions that rely on relational health principles in addressing obesity, opioid use disorder, and depression in the elderly. This chapter expands on those programmatic ideas by identifying how relational health can broadly inform policy priorities. In doing so, it addresses the central question of how to incorporate the "four socials" into national health policy – specifically, how these relational factors inform health prevention efforts and health care delivery. The policy priorities all emerge from the evidence that social relationships significantly impact our health and the quality of our lives.

The recommendations in this chapter are designed to provide a roadmap for relational health initiatives. They are necessarily preliminary, since more research in relational health interventions is needed before advocating for specific programs. The recommendations here reflect insights derived from expert analyses who, having evaluated the operation and financing of the health care system, have identified reforms needed to achieve better health outcomes for these major health concerns. These include strengthening social and health care integration, mobilizing community resources, and enhancing workforce skills training.

Better Integrated Social and Medical Services

First, we must visualize a policy shift away from what we have now, which is a health care system designed to treat patients individually without much regard for social context and the role of social supports. Structuring and financing health care along these principles have led to the world's most expensive health care system and one of the developed world's least effective. In his book *More than Medicine*,[1] Dr. Robert Kaplan, former Chief Science Officer at the US Agency for Healthcare Research and Quality (AHRQ) and Associate Director of the National Institutes of Health, emphasizes that we need to shift our thinking away from the long-held conviction that more health care is better to instead recognize that improving quality of life should be our primary goal. To achieve a better quality of life, more social services are needed. He urges a reshaping of priorities in how we invest resources: "Policy makers should be thinking hard about how to expand social services, even if doing so might result in diverting resources from healthcare."

Social services are traditionally designed to support many drivers of good health, including housing, safety, and food insecurity. They also include relational health services that provide critical social and community support, such as infrastructure needs, community health workers, and a host of other services that are oriented toward leveraging relationships to improve health, many of which are discussed in Chapter 5. Despite how critical these services are for improving health and wellbeing, they have historically been woefully underfunded.

Kaplan provides evidence that relatively modest investments in these services can have big effects on the life expectancies and quality of life in the United States. According to the Centers for Medicare & Medicaid Services, most of the nation's health care spending ($3.8 trillion) in 2019 was spent to finance hospitals, physicians, and clinics.[2] Of the total monies invested, hospital care consumes 31 percent; physician and clinical services, 20 percent; prescription drugs, 10 percent; dental and other professionals, 7 percent; government administration, 8 percent; nursing and long-term care, 5 percent; investment (equipment, research, structures), 5 percent; and 14 percent is for "other" costs, which include medical equipment, medical products, home health care, public health activities, and other health residential and personal care (residential care facilities, ambulance

[1] Kaplan, R. M. (2019). *More than Medicine.* Harvard University Press.
[2] Centers for Medicare & Medicaid Services. (2019). *The Nation's Health Dollar ($3.8 Trillion), Calendar Year 2019: Where It Came From.* Centers for Medicare & Medicaid Services.

providers, medical care delivered in nontraditional settings such as schools, community centers, senior citizen centers, and military field stations, and expenditures for Home and Community waiver programs under Medicaid). Other scholars have found that health outcomes improve when more money is devoted toward these types of services.[3] In an analysis of the rate of public spending on health and social services in each state from 2000 to 2009, Yale researchers Elizabeth Bradley and colleagues, found that the states that had a higher ratio of social and health spending also had better health outcomes one and two years later, compared to states with lower ratios.

A Change of Priorities

The findings from Bradley's research team suggest that a different prioritization of investments in social services and public health, not just investment in health care, may be an important part of improving health outcomes and reducing variations across the states. They also suggest the potential of changing policies nationwide. When extended across the US population, the magnitude of the effects they found was substantial. For example, a 20 percent change in the median ratio of social to health spending was associated with a −0.33-percentage-point change in the percentage of adults with obesity in the subsequent year. The researchers calculated that, at the time, when there were approximately 78 million obese adults nationwide in 2009, the effect of such a change would have been 85,000 fewer adults with obesity. Obesity is staggeringly higher now than in 2009.

Integrating social services and health care both improves outcomes and lowers health care costs.[4] While there are many examples in practice where social services have been included in health care models, these efforts tend to be limited to small-scale pilot studies. To date, only a few organizations have moved beyond temporary grant funding to a more sustainable long-term model of integration. Performance measures that evaluate return on investment – that is, the financial gain or loss generated relative to the amount spent – argue that the integration of social services is a smart investment strategy for health care organizations and should be more

[3] Bradley, E. H., Canavan, M., Rogan, E., et al. (2016). Variation in health outcomes: the role of spending on social services, public health, and health care, 2000–09. *Health Affairs* 35(5): 760–768. https://doi.org/10.1377/hlthaff.2015.0814

[4] Commonwealth Fund. (2018). *Investing in Social Services as a Core Strategy for Healthcare Organizations: Developing the Business Case*. Commonwealth Fund.

widely pursued. A 2018 Commonwealth Fund report concludes that initial social service investments yield strong financial returns within a time frame of eighteen months or shorter.

For these reasons, health care organizations have been urged to pursue concrete steps toward making and communicating an organizational commitment to addressing health-related social needs at the community and individual levels.[5] Strategies to integrate relational care into the delivery of health care can take different forms, and a focus toward relational health provides direction on where social service investments can make the most difference. One approach is "social prescribing," which refers to the ways in which health care providers assess social needs, determine when support services are necessary, and refer patients to appropriate services. Referrals are done by connecting patients with community assets (typically voluntary or charitable organizations) that provide social and personal support.

Social prescribing can improve patients' health and wellbeing by attending to their nonclinical needs.[6] It is already widespread in the United Kingdom and has become a mainstream National Health Service provision. Even with the very different health system in the United States, there are approaches that have been developed to provide similar services. However, according to leaders in the field of social prescribing, we are now at a point where, "despite the strong evidence linking adverse social conditions to health outcomes, little is known about what the healthcare sector should do about them," a sentiment that underscores the need for social and health care integrated services.[7]

The rationale for social and health care integration is that unaddressed social needs cannot be ignored in patient care. At the same time, health care providers and large health care systems that have been slow to integrate acknowledge they do not have the capacity or ability to address patients' social needs. One solution is for providers and health systems to work in

---

[5] National Academies of Sciences, Engineering, and Medicine. (2019). *Integrating Social Care into the Delivery of Health Care: Moving Upstream to Improve the Nation's Health.* The National Academies Press. https://doi.org/10.17226/25467

[6] Brown, R. C. H., Mahtani, K., Turk, A., & Tierney, S. (2021). Social prescribing in national health service primary care: what are the ethical considerations? *Milbank Quarterly 99*(3): 610–628. https://doi.org/10.1111/1468-0009.12516; Alderwick, H. A. J., Gottlieb, L. M., Fichtenberg, C. M., & Adler, N. E. (2018). Social prescribing in the U.S. and England: emerging interventions to address patients' social needs. *American Journal of Preventive Medicine 54*(5): 715–718. https://doi.org/10.1016/j.amepre.2018.01.039

[7] Gottlieb, L. M., DeSalvo, K., & Adler, N. E. (2019). Healthcare sector activities to identify and intervene on social risk: an introduction to the American Journal of Preventive Medicine supplement. *American Journal of Preventive Medicine 57*(6): S1–S5. https://doi.org/10.1016/j.amepre.2019.07.009

partnership with community-based organizations and other entities to develop effective care. Models for how to achieve better integration are still developing, but several models have already shown promising health improvements for their participants.

One example is Geisinger Health Systems, which is an integrated health services organization in Pennsylvania that serves patients across Medicare, Medicaid, and commercial insurance plans. Geisinger launched a "Fresh Food Farmacy" in 2016 for patients with type 2 diabetes, for which obesity is a major risk factor.[8] Participants in the program meet with a comprehensive care team that includes dieticians, wellness coaches, and social workers that provides recipes and demonstrations for how to prepare healthy meals, connect with providers, and provide other needed resources. Participants are also expected to attend an evidence-based weekly diabetes self-management program. Through partnerships with local food organizations, and primarily the Central Pennsylvania Food Bank, the Fresh Food Farmacy can provide up to ten meals a week of fresh, healthy food to patients and their households. Since launching in 2016, data from Fresh Food Farmacy patients show an average two-point drop in HbA1c levels (a measure of blood sugar attached to hemoglobin that is used as a biomarker for diabetes), along with lower weight, blood pressure, triglycerides, and cholesterol. Data also shows a collective $1.5 million in health care savings for Geisinger patients who have participated in the program.

Among the more recent changes in the health care landscape is payment reform. Here, altered payment structures have been successful in encouraging health care providers and health care systems to pay more attention to how social factors influence their patients' health outcomes. Traditional fee-for-service payment models that pay health care providers a fee for each service that they deliver, which incentivizes high-volume and high-price health care regardless of whether patients benefit, are being replaced with value-based care models.

Simply put, integrated care will only thrive where quality is emphasized and rewarded over quantity. In value-based care, public and private payers hold providers (e.g., physicians and hospitals) accountable for patients' health and health care costs, and in doing so they link payments to outcomes. Figure 6.1 illustrates the intended benefits – lower health care costs, higher patient satisfaction, and reduced risks – of this type of model.

---

[8] Fresh Food Farmacy. (2021). Fresh Food Farmacy. Retrieved from: www.geisinger.org /freshfoodfarmacy

Value-Based Health Care Benefits

PATIENTS	PROVIDERS	PAYERS	SUPPLIERS	SOCIETY
Lower costs and better outcomes	Higher patient satisfaction rates and better care efficiencies	Stronger cost controls and reduced risks	Alignment of prices with patient outcomes	Reduced health care spending and better overall health

Figure 6.1 Value-based health care benefits. Adapted from NEJM Catalyst (catalyst. nejm.org) © Massachusetts Medical Society.[9]

The complexities of the value-based care financial structure are beyond the scope of this book, but its underlying motivations align with the possibility of implementing relational health. Value-based models create economic incentives for providers to incorporate social interventions into their approach to care. For example, for chronic diseases such as obesity, providers are encouraged to focus on prevention and avoidance of disease before it starts, so that hospitalizations and costly tests and procedures can be avoided. In addition, these models encourage structural changes to address fragmented care, in which different health care providers do not effectively work together in the management of care, and instead provide more integrated medical and social services. Patient-centered medical homes, for example, have developed as part of value-based care.

Health care organizations might also expand relational care to fulfill the obligations of nonprofit health care delivery systems to earn their tax-exempt status. Much of providers' relational care may be run through community benefit programs, and health care organizations can bring funds, data, and political and other forms of capital to catalyze community activities. The health care sector has not consistently wielded this capital in the interest of primary prevention of clinical conditions or prevention of the complicating social conditions.[10]

Health care providers are encouraged to follow the accumulated evidence for best practices for screening for social risk factors and social needs. These include standardized and validated questions (see details on PRAPARE in Chapter 5) that can be contained within data systems such as EPIC in order to

---

[9] NEJM Catalyst (2017). What is value-based healthcare? *NEJM Catalyst*. Retrieved from: https://catalyst.nejm.org/doi/full/10.1056/CAT.17.0558.

[10] National Academies of Sciences, Engineering, and Medicine. (2019). *Integrating Social Care into the Delivery of Health Care: Moving Upstream to Improve the Nation's Health*. The National Academies Press. https://doi.org/10.17226/25467

maintain a more comprehensive patient record. When patients are screened for social risks, those with identified needs can then be connected to appropriate social services. In doing so, the health care system can serve a valuable role, for example, in identifying risk for social isolation and then connecting patients with social care or community programs. Several state Medicaid plans and private insurers have launched programs that are more intentionally designed to address social isolation and loneliness. For example, health care organizations could partner with ride-sharing programs to enable older adults to travel to medical appointments and community events.

In screening for social risk, care management efforts can face the "bridge to nowhere" problem in which patients are assessed for needs but then find that services are not available to address those needs. One response has been "personalized community referral platforms" that maintain updated records of community resources. These kinds of platforms can be integrated with electronic health records and can automate referrals – for example, if a bilingual substance use support group is needed for a patient, the health care provider can use this platform to identify where one may be that is close to the patient's home address. Despite the potential of such services, patients are often referred to places that do not have the capacity to provide what is required. The priority should be facilitating and supporting partnerships between health systems and community organizations to care for patients who require social services.

Health care organizations have also developed integration capabilities whereby needed support services are provided "in house." This can be achieved through a model of primary care called patient-centered medical homes.[11] These models of care address patients' physical and mental health care needs, including prevention and wellness, acute care, and chronic care. They are designed to provide comprehensive care, often through a team of care providers. A team might include physicians, advanced practice nurses, physician assistants, nurses, pharmacists, nutritionists, social workers, educators, and care coordinators. These care models may provide their services all in one place, a one-stop-shop, or for smaller practices they may refer out to care.

One example of this type of in-house care is Mary's Center, a community health center based in Washington, DC that provides comprehensive, integrated care for low-resourced communities.[12] The operating principle for Mary's Center is that treating someone's physical health in isolation from

[11] PCMH Resource Center. (2021). Defining the PCMH. Retrieved from: https://pcmh.ahrq.gov/page/defining-pcmh.
[12] www.maryscenter.org.

their complex individual, family, and community contexts is insufficient to improve their overall wellbeing. The center has progressively expanded its service offerings over thirty years, evolving from providing traditional medical services to adopting a more sophisticated delivery model that meets a range of medical and nonmedical needs in-house. Its staff is now equipped with strong connections across service areas. For example, when a caregiver brings their child to Mary's Center for a wellness visit, they may be asked about their own medical or mental health needs. A medical provider can then introduce a participant to other medical, dental, or social services providers within Mary's Center, or provide a referral for additional services with one of its partners.

For opioid use disorder, integrating social care with health care delivery can address the co-occurring mental health disorders and trauma that often make recovery so challenging. Despite a wide range of effective addiction treatments currently available, only 20 percent of people who need treatment receive necessary care. As discussed in previous chapters, misinformation, lack of information, and stigmatization of substance use hampers progress in providing available (and successful) treatment to those who need it.

Multidisciplinary integrated pain management programs can significantly reduce the burden of poorly managed pain, which is associated with opioid use and misuse. Integrated pain management programs can include pharmacological treatment, as well as nonpharmacological treatments like physical therapy, yoga, and meditation, all of which are available through a variety of providers.

Veterans Affairs (VA) has done some exemplary work around integrated pain management. The US Department of Veteran's Affairs Whole Health System is an example of a successful implementation of an integrated health approach.[13] The Whole Health System is a systemic, person-centered approach to providing comprehensive health care, and it is designed to take shape early in the relationship between the VA and the veteran. While the system is not specific to pain management, chronic pain management is a frequent focus. Unlike traditional episodic care models, this system is designed for continuous engagement with the veteran throughout life. The model emphasizes self-care within the broader context of wellbeing and incorporates a full range of conventional and

---

[13] Bokhour, B. G., Haun, J. N., Hyde, J., Charns, M., & Kligler, B. (2020). Transforming the Veterans Affairs to a whole health system of care: time for action and research. *Medical Care* 58(4): 295–300. https://doi.org/10.1097/MLR.0000000000001316

complementary and integrative health approaches, including stress reduction, yoga, tai chi, mindfulness, nutrition, acupuncture, and health coaching.

Another successful emerging model is medication-assisted treatment (MAT) programs, which combine behavioral therapy with the careful use of milder opiates to prevent withdrawal symptoms.[14] The combination of self-help support groups with monitored medication has been shown to produce improved treatment outcomes such as lowering the likelihood of returning to substance use. Community efforts to harmonize self-help and medication treatment warrant continued support. As more Medicaid programs cover recovery support services, including self-help groups, incentivizing the development of self-help peer recovery programs that embrace medication treatment is important. More attention needs to be paid to building that evidence base, which will help guide resource allocation decisions.

Strengthening social and health care integration can also include providing legal support and counseling. Medical legal partnerships (MLP) involve lawyers that are embedded on-site in clinical settings and work as part of a team with health care providers to address patients' health-harming legal problems. Nationally, more than 300 health care organizations operate MLPs, and many more are in the planning stage. General hospitals and health systems, Federally Qualified Health Centers, veteran's health systems, private and nonprofit community clinics, and other specialty health care providers now include MLP services in their operations.

Medical legal partnerships can function as one critical recovery service alongside medical treatment and other supportive services. For pregnant women with substance use disorder (SUD), treatment is not just insufficient and fragmented, but it is also punishable by law. By 2017, a total of twenty-six states had implemented punitive policies that classify prenatal substance use as a form of child abuse or neglect and evidence of maternal use can lead to fines, jail time, and loss of custody. Instead of drawing women into care and helping them recover, these policies push them away from care and into the criminal justice system. Research indicates that pregnant women who use substances tend to isolate themselves, miss prenatal care appointments, or avoid medical care altogether when they feel threatened by the potential for detection or punishment. Emerging

---

[14] SAMHSA (n.d.). Medication-assisted treatment (MAT). Retrieved from: www.samhsa.gov/medication-assisted-treatment

evidence suggests that punitive laws harm or fail to help infants and mothers, with some women avoiding substance use treatment and rates of neonatal abstinence syndrome either increasing or remaining unchanged in states with such policies.[15]

A case study from the MLP at Eskenazi Health Midtown Community Mental Health in Indianapolis, Indiana, demonstrates how offering legal services can support recovery and help individuals thrive when delivered in tandem with health and behavioral health care.

Case Study 6.1: Jamie[16]

"Jamie" is an individual with an opioid-related SUD. Jaime's daughter was born with opioids in her system and was consequently placed in foster care by the state child welfare agency as a newborn. When her child was taken away, Jamie committed to recovery. She enrolled in a MAT program, which combined therapy with replacement opioids to prevent withdrawal. MAT worked for Jamie, and she remained clean and committed to treatment for almost a year, at which time the child welfare agency recommended that she regain full custody of her daughter. At the final placement hearing, however, the judge demanded that she "wean" off her MAT because the judge viewed it as merely, "replacing one addiction with another," a common stigma and misconception about MAT. Jamie was referred by her health care provider to the health center's on-site MLP. The MLP attorney wrote a letter with Jamie's treatment team explaining that: (1) ending MAT was a purely medical decision that could only be made by Jamie's doctor; and (2) Jamie was thriving in recovery and committed to staying clean. This letter was presented to the judge, who changed her mind and awarded Jamie full, permanent custody of her now two-year-old daughter.

Studies to date suggest that social needs interventions improve health outcomes and patient experience of care while reducing avoidable health services use and associated costs, but more research is needed to understand the mechanisms by which these interventions may work. It may be that by addressing social needs, care quality is improved, which can reduce patient stress and may also reduce provider burnout and

---

[15] Haffajee, R. L., Faherty, L. J., & Zivin, K. (2021). Pregnant women with substance use disorders: the harm associated with punitive approaches. *New England Journal of Medicine* 384(25): 2364–2367. https://doi.org/10.1056/NEJMp2101051

[16] Chaudhary, J., Marple, K., & Bajema, J. (2018). The opioid crisis in America & the role medical-legal partnership can play in recovery. Issue brief. National Center for Medical Legal Partnerships.

turnover.[17] Designing and implementing integrated care systems should engage patients, community partners, frontline staff, social care workers, and clinicians in the planning and evaluation. Incorporating the preferences of patients, providers, and communities in program planning and execution would ensure that the needs of all relevant stakeholders are being addressed.

Relational Health Policy Priorities for Prevention of Disease: Improve Community Assets

We have much more to gain from preventing disease than from treating it once it has taken hold. In her book *Elderhood*, Louise Aronson perfectly summarizes a fundamental principle of population health science: "Although American health care prioritizes its money and efforts into treatment, prevention is unequivocally the better approach economically, medically, and morally, since it keeps people from getting sick and needing medical care in the first place."[18]

But how does relational health advance efforts at prevention? A relational health approach teaches that demanding individuals make behavior changes is destined to disappoint. The same is true for any kind of health program that requires people to draw on extensive personal resources, including time, money, or willpower. These kinds of programs are unlikely to be sustainable or equitable if inadequate support is provided to those who need it.

A relational health approach instead calls for prevention-focused policies that mobilize community resources, such as public space and communication infrastructure, that advance individual health needs.[19] Investments in community resources tend to be absent in health spending budgets, but there are enormous population health benefits when spaces serve as centers of social interaction. To be most effective, prevention efforts should happen alongside additional efforts that leverage support networks and community-based treatments. Effective policies are needed that can bridge the gaps between health care and other sectors of the economy that focus

[17] Fichtenberg, C. M., Alley, D. E., & Mistry, K. B. (2019). Improving social needs intervention research: key questions for advancing the field. *American Journal of Preventive Medicine* 57(6): S47–S54. https://doi.org/10.1016/j.amepre.2019.07.018

[18] Aronson, L. (2019). *Elderhood*. Bloomsbury.

[19] Goulbourne, T., & Yanovitzky, I. (2021). The communication infrastructure as a social determinant of health: implications for health policymaking and practice. *Milbank Quarterly* 99(1): 24–40. https://doi.org/10.1111/1468-0009.12496

on preventive care. Programs and policies should emphasize recognizing and prioritizing access to social connection in addition to access to fresh food, exercise, and other conditions that are all necessary for health and wellbeing.

For obesity, this means strategies that are focused on buffering against factors that promote unhealthy consumption patterns and provide ongoing support opportunities. Substance use policy needs to reflect that a significant driver of opioids abuse stems from emotional pain – isolation, trauma, unaddressed mental health needs – and that stress can cause relapses. Social supports, stability, and connections to one's community can help build the resiliency in individuals that is critical for recovery. To mitigate social isolation among the elderly, policymakers need to be attentive to the built environment and to designing age-friendly communities that create social networks within the elder community.[20]

There are also vast needs to invest in enabling older people to age in place. Policy priorities should be focused on both preserving and creating public venues where older people can meet. As noted by sociologists and public health experts, at this point most policy recommendations for reducing isolation are only speculative. "We lack sound research on the effectiveness of proposed interventions for social isolation, in different contexts and with different populations."[21] To truly improve social isolation, interventions need to consider structural changes, not only individual-level interventions, that can promote community, including investment in public spaces that will serve as centralized locations for the elderly to build and maintain social networks. The physical needs of the elderly are too often prioritized at the expense of their social needs, which can be equally important.

Health Care Workforce Improvements

The relational approach also encourages us to rethink how network support can be incorporated into treatment plans. This in turn forces us to rethink some aspects of health care delivery. In order to incorporate relational and behavioral principles into health care delivery, health care providers need to have the skills to offer those services. There are three

[20] Fulmer, T., Reuben, D. B., Auerbach, J., et al. (2021). Actualizing better health and health care for older adults. *Health Affairs* 40(2): 219–225. https://doi.org/10.1377/hlthaff.2020.01470

[21] Klinenberg, E. (2016). Social isolation, loneliness, and living alone: identifying the risks for public health. *American Journal of Public Health* 106(5): 786–787. https://doi.org/10.2105/AJPH.2016.303166

main policy priorities that pertain to the health care workforce: changes to training and education, increasing the quantity of community health and peer recovery providers, and paying for nonmedical personnel.

A relational health approach forces a rethinking of how we train our health care workforce.[22] Medical and nursing schools rarely train physicians and nurses to consider how relational factors influence health. Health care providers should have a working knowledge of how the "four socials" play important roles in many chronic health conditions, how social support can promote wellness, and how to utilize peer resources and community norms for behavioral interventions.

One reason these relational dynamics have been excluded from medical professional education is the pressure to specialize. Specialization discourages the introduction of relational health principles on the belief that it is the exclusive domain of social workers. Specialization also erects a barrier to integrated care by inhibiting team-based models of care.[23] Training specialists in relational health principals may remove some of the barriers.

Team-based primary care, in which at least two health providers work collaboratively with patients and communities to accomplish shared health goals, has led to some of the most effective practices. Team-based care emphasizes fostering positive relationships with patients and develops practices that enhance integration of medical and social care. Among the best practices developed are the "warm handoff" and cultural competency.

Warm handoffs describe a practice in which one team member who has a relationship with the patient directs a patient to work with another team member, explains why the other team member can address a patient's specific concern, emphasizes the other team member's competence, asks for the patient's acceptance of the plan, and then "hands off" that patient to the other provider, either personally or via referral. When the original team member describes the other team member positively and tells the patient how the other staff member will help meet the patient's needs, the colleague is not only transferring trust to the other provider, but also helping the patient to see the team as a coherent, identifiable group. This practice builds a sense of cohesion, identity, and trust among the team and with patients.

[22] Doobay-Persaud, A., Adler, M. D., Bartell, T. R., et al. (2019). Teaching the social determinants of health in undergraduate medical education: a scoping review. *Journal of General Internal Medicine* 34(5): 720–730. https://doi.org/10.1007/s11606-019-04876-0

[23] Dower, C., Moore, J., & Langelier, M. (2013). It Is time to restructure health professions scope-of-practice regulations to remove barriers to care. *Health Affairs* 32(11): 1971–1976. https://doi.org/10.1377/hlthaff.2013.0537

Providing culturally appropriate care calls for prioritizing training in cultural competence for all staff to ensure that care is attentive to patients' needs and values.[24] Such training can enhance understanding of the health care experiences of patients with diverse backgrounds and improve skills to effectively work in cross-cultural situations.

Health care providers would also benefit from more training in the care of older people, and specifically in the recognition and management of social isolation. Training programs for direct care workers such as home health aides, nurse aides, and personal care aides should also incorporate social isolation and loneliness in their curricula.[25] In order to improve outcomes, health professionals need to learn core content in areas such as the health impacts of social isolation and loneliness, assessment strategies, and referral options and processes.[26]

Comprehensive addiction training is similarly lacking in medical education. The stigma associated with opioid use disorder can discourage health care professionals from wanting to work with a patient population that is viewed as incurable or manipulative. To address issues of reluctance to treat this patient population among the broader medical system, state and federal entities need to do more to educate the broader medical provider community about treating patients with opioid use disorder, including issuing guidelines, engaging providers in educational and training opportunities, and ensuring that reimbursement rates are sufficient to provide care for what are often complex patients.[27]

Scaling up the quantity of community health and peer recovery providers is another essential workforce improvement policy priority. Community health workers are trusted members of the communities they serve and can play a unique and valuable role as part of health care teams. They increase access to preventive services, facilitate system navigation, provide care coordination for chronic disease management, and act as

[24] Khanna, S., Cheyney, M., & Engle, M. (2009). Cultural competency in health care: evaluating the outcomes of a cultural competency training among health care professionals. *Journal of the National Medical Association* 101(9): 886–892. https://doi.org/10.1016/S0027-9684(15)31035-X

[25] National Academies of Science, Engineering, and Medicine. (2019). Integrating social needs care into the delivery of health care to improve the nation's health. Retrieved from: www .nationalacademies.org/our-work/integrating-social-needs-care-into-the-delivery-of-health-care-to-improve-the-nations-health

[26] National Academies of Sciences, Engineering, and Medicine, Integrating Social Care into the Delivery of Health Care.

[27] Clemans-Cope, L., Wishner, J. B., Allen, E. H., et al. (2017). Experiences of three states implementing the Medicaid health home model to address opioid use disorder: case studies in Maryland, Rhode Island, and Vermont. *Journal of Substance Abuse Treatment* 83: 27–35. https://doi.org/10.1016/j.jsat.2017.10.001

important connectors with the health care system and the broader community. For opioid use disorder, for example, including peers in a behavioral health workforce reduces substance use and relapse rates. It also improves social support and increases treatment retention and patient satisfaction, and provides hope across diverse patient samples.[28]

In a series of policy briefs on the value of community health workers, FamiliesUSA, a nonpartisan consumer health advocacy organization, stated that "As policymakers at the state and federal levels look for opportunities to transform healthcare delivery and promote equity, the effective, systematic use of community health workers can be a game changer, and should be integrated into system transformation efforts."[29] To maximize community health workers' effectiveness, states should work to integrate community health workers into the "care team" of physicians, nurses, and other providers that are involved in patient care. This encourages comprehensive care plans that consider both individual and community needs and allows the care team to provide a broader range of support. Some managed care organizations have partnered with state Medicaid programs, health care providers, and others to test innovative ways of integrating community health workers into delivering care. One case study highlighted in the FamiliesUSA brief showed how New Mexico's Medicaid program has promoted the use of community health workers within its managed care organizations, and these workers offer a broad scope of services including chronic disease management, counseling, health literacy, and connection with non-health-care supportive services.[30]

Another urgent workforce reform is to expand the definition for billable providers, especially for roles like community health workers and case managers – which can be of critical importance in addressing the needs of patients most burdened by chronic illness and the high costs of avoidable emergency department use and hospitalizations. This could be achieved through reimbursement policies that recognize and reward these services.

[28] Alegría, M., Frank, R. G., Hansen, H. B., et al. (2021). Transforming mental health and addiction services. *Health Affairs* 40(2): 226–234. https://doi.org/10.1377/hlthaff.2020.01472

[29] Hernández-Cancio, S., Houshyar, S., & Walawender, M. (2018, September). Community health workers: key partners in improving children's health and eliminating inequities. Families USA. Retrieved from www.orchwa.org/resources/Documents/HE_CHWs-and-Kids_Issue-Brief.pdf.

[30] Albritton, E. (2016, July). How states can fund community health workers through Medicaid to improve people's health, decrease costs, and reduce disparities. Families USA. Retrieved from https://familiesusa.org/wp-content/uploads/2019/09/HE_HST_Community_Health_Workers_Brief_v4.pdf.

Conclusion

Our current health crises suggest a need for bold policy solutions that prioritize nonmedical investments. This chapter grapples with policy priorities that can best implement and sustain relational health principles. The lessons from relational health inform specific elements of social policy, some of which are departures from current practice, and some of which involve modest changes in emphasis; some have been long urged by commentators and policy experts, and some are less intuitive. They all reflect the importance of social relationships for our health. The policy priorities described in this chapter envision a future that invests in preventive care, community resources, and the integration of social and physical health. It is a strategy to ensure that fewer people get sick and more people achieve and sustain a higher quality of life. And when people do find a need for health care, they encounter providers who are trained in identifying crucial nonmedical needs and can connect patients with services and support.

Prior health policy reforms have prioritized reforming the health care industry by creating more efficiencies and reducing wasteful spending. These are essential objectives, but it will not achieve population health benefits if there are inadequate social services to protect against disease. Maintaining the current system of medicalizing social problems and expecting health care providers (and the larger health care system) to treat illness that stems from unmet social needs is untenable. A relational health approach instead suggests that social and health care need to be better integrated.

Policy solutions include structural changes that promote community. Physical and social environments can play a significant role in the healthy aging of older adults. Communication infrastructure refers to formal and informal communication channels and networks that enable regular interactions between community members and other people outside of the community.

Policy approaches must acknowledge individual agency and recognize that people should take ultimate responsibility for their own health. At the same time, these approaches must also recognize that numerous factors can support or undermine individuals' ability to act in their own self-interest. This is especially true for "low agency" populations – those who have few personal resources – who need help implementing strategies to pursue better health. Combating obesity and opioid use and implementing isolation-reduction strategies require employing the most powerful levers for systemic change. These comprehensive approaches are the strategies that are the most likely to tackle these daunting health concerns.

CHAPTER 7

Conclusions

At the writing of this final chapter the world is still in the grips of the COVID-19 pandemic that began in January 2020. Vaccines are being distributed unevenly across the world and, although normalcy in everyday life is only starting to resume, there are lessons to be taken from our shared realities so far. One consequence of the stay-at-home orders and physical distancing required to contain the spread of the coronavirus is that we have gained some valuable insights about the critical role of our social networks. Normal routines that would put people in contact with one another were no longer possible and negative health effects of social isolation grew as a consequence. One study relying on survey data reported that individuals of all ages felt isolated during the pandemic and subsequently experienced a range of negative effects: low life satisfaction, work-related stress, lower trust of institutions (e.g., central government and business), less connection to community, lower satisfaction with environmental factors (e.g., housing and food), and higher levels of substance use as a coping strategy.[1]

Social isolation during COVID was also associated with negative population-wide effects on the three health outcomes that are the focus of this book. According to new data from the CDC, obesity rates increased,[2] and this magnified the impact of COVID since obese patients exhibited higher rates of hospitalization and mortality from the virus. Opioid overdose deaths also spiked during the pandemic. A summary published by the American Medical Association in August 2021 reported that there was a spike or increase in overdose deaths during the COVID pandemic *in*

---

[1] Clair, R., Gordon, M., Kroon, M., et al. (2021). The effects of social isolation on well-being and life satisfaction during pandemic. *Humanities and Social Science Communications* 28. https://doi.org/10.1057/s41599-021-00710-3

[2] Centers for Disease Control and Prevention (2020, September 17). Coronavirus Disease 2019. Retrieved from: www.cdc.gov/media/releases/2020/s0917-adult-obesity-increasing.html

every state in the United States.[3] And many older adults, especially those who lacked access to smart technology and were distanced from family and friends, had fewer social resources to cope with the stress of COVID.[4] Their limited ability to engage in physical exercise or other interactive routines required also exacerbated their mental health challenges.

We have also learned valuable lessons from the meaningful investments that were made in community safety nets and public resources, many of which yielded significant benefits during the COVID pandemic. In Milwaukee, Wisconsin, for example, Children's Wisconsin health care system quickly established a telehealth program for mental health and substance abuse when it realized that both children and adults exhibited greater needs for behavioral therapy over the course of the pandemic. It has received more than 30,000 virtual visits since April 2020. Counseling programs for youth that required home visits prior to COVID transitioned to curbside face-to-face visits outside youths' homes and virtual visits.[5] And it collaborated with Milwaukee County and three other Milwaukee health systems to create a new mental health emergency center that is part of a $150 million, five-year plan for addressing the growing mental health and substance use crisis. In response to similarly growing needs for adults, the Milwaukee Behavioral Health Division partnered with community health centers to expand behavioral health and health care services on the north and east sides of Milwaukee.

As the world moves forward in its recovery from the pandemic, an increased awareness of our interdependency should encourage an intentional building of connection and community that will be an essential part of the collective healing process.[6] This means following successful program examples as described in Chapter 5, including strategies that effectively integrate social networks into how we care for these particular health crises, with programmatic examples of how social connectedness can facilitate and support behavior change. Programs that can be incorporated into practice and provide sustained benefits are the

[3] American Medical Association Advocacy Resource Center (2021). Issue brief: Nation's drug-related overdose and death epidemic continues to worsen. Retrieved from: www.ama-assn.org/system/files/issue-brief-increases-in-opioid-related-overdose.pdf.

[4] Vahia, I. V., Jeste, D. V., & Reynolds, C. F. (2020). Older adults and the mental health effects of COVID-19. *JAMA* 324(22): 2253–2254. https://doi.org/10.1001/jama.2020.21753

[5] Children's Wisconsin (n.d.). Strong families, thriving children. Retrieved from: https://childrenswi.org/childrens-and-the-community/community-partners-professionals/strong-families.

[6] Marill, M. C. (2019). Beyond twelve steps, peer-supported mental health care. *Health Affairs* 38(6): 896–901. https://doi.org/10.1377/hlthaff.2019.00503

best direction, although continued work is needed to determine who benefits the most – and least – from these interventions, and then to tailor them as needed.

A Long-Term Relational Health Strategy

Relational factors need to be incorporated into long-term health strategies that will help prevent and mitigate health crises. Relational health suggests a set of priorities for how we organize our society and build connections between individuals and communities. We can draw inspiration for "an alternative moral vision of public health" from Native American responses, which have centered community and existing networks of connections to successfully implement mitigation and vaccination measures in response to COVID.[7] We currently have an opportunity to reshape our language, culture, and attitudes on health and wellbeing in valuable ways.

Prevention

Prevention is a key theme underlying population health science and has specific meaning for relational health. Relational health strategies point to the necessity of maintaining social resources in communities that contribute to healthy behaviors and lifestyles. The American Rescue Plan has brought historic funding to local communities to address pressing issues, and these communities exercised significant discretion over how funds are used and have approached their responses in different ways. According to a report by the Robert Wood Johnson Foundation, positive impacts of investments in infrastructure and support building have been found in diverse communities across the country, such as: Finney County, Kansas; Harris County, Texas; Milwaukee, Wisconsin; Mobile, Alabama; and San Juan County, New Mexico.[8] More opportunities to build on these positive examples and expand these kinds of programming to other communities are needed. Bearing relational factors in mind when designing

---

[7] Tomori, C., Ahmed, A., Evans, D. P., Meier, B. M., & Nair, A. (2021). Your health is in your hands? US CDC COVID-19 mask guidance reveals the moral foundations of public health. *EClinicalMedicine* 38: 101071. https://doi.org/10.1016/j.eclinm.2021.101071. PBS NewsHour (2020, April 24). Navajo Nation, hit hard by COVID-19, comes together to protect its most vulnerable. Retrieved from: www.pbs.org/newshour/show/navajo-nation-hit-hard-by-covid-19-comes-together-to-protect-its-most-vulnerable

[8] Robert Wood Johnson Foundation (2020, July 27). COVID-19 community response: emerging themes across sentinel communities. Retrieved from: www.rwjf.org/en/library/interactives/covid-19-community-response--emerging-themes-across-sentinel-communities.html.

communities for the elderly can serve to reduce social isolation. Creating public spaces that provide opportunities for social engagement can reduce isolation, and supportive housing enables the elderly to "age in place" and maintain the social fabric of their communities.

Mitigation

Relational factors also play an essential role in mitigating these health crises. Mitigation strategies include social support groups, peer-recovery support services, and "place-based strategies" that create social networks within the community and help to secure long-term services and supports. Relational health suggests priorities for expanding the availability and quality of support services and the uptake of alternative models for delivery, such as telehealth. Other mitigation strategies include improved case management and connection to social service supports. For example, several effective tools are available to identify youth, adults, and families at risk for substance misuse and mental health concerns. Models like Accountable Health Communities and Nurse Family Partnerships help support systems for identification, referral, connection to care, and follow-up. Other useful strategies include the greater use of community health workers and peer-counselor and support models where appropriate.

Provision of Care

Some visionary community-based health care initiatives developed during COVID and the ensuing recovery provide more promising examples of relational health approaches at work. CARE2HOPE (Kentucky Communities and Researchers Engaging to Halt the Opioid Epidemic), led by epidemiologist Dr. April Young, draws on inherent sources of resilience that can be tapped in some rural eastern Kentucky communities. Young says, "The social connectedness can be a real strength . . . Often these families have lived in these communities for generations, and so there's a strong connection to place. That can be a strength and a real sense of pride. Those are all, I think, really important forces for potentially shaping better health outcomes."[9] Young, reflecting on those eastern Kentucky communities where she has spent time, talks not about the gaps, but about how to leverage those long-standing strengths – from deep roots to strong kinship networks.

---

[9] Huff, C. (2020). Confronting an opioid crisis and promoting health from all angles. *Health Affairs* 39 (11): 1861–1866. https://doi.org/10.1377/hlthaff.2020.01667

The rise of peer supported mental health care – a program that is deeply rooted in the principles of relational health – is "a bright spot in an otherwise strained behavioral health system," according to a report on a peer provider program in Georgia.[10] By 2030, the United States is projected to have a shortage of 5,000–10,000 psychiatrists, depending on assumptions about demand, according to a 2018 analysis by the Health Resources and Services Administration (HRSA). The HRSA predicts shortages in most states for other behavioral health workers as well, including psychologists, social workers, and addiction counselors. By definition, peer-support providers are nonclinical and cannot fill the gap of other mental health professionals. But increasingly, peer specialists work in programs designed to avert crises. For example, the Georgia Mental Health Consumer Network runs a 24/7 "warm line" that offers people phone support – a way to connect with someone with lived experience who can provide encouragement, resources, and emotional support. For a mental health emergency, peer-support providers can transfer people to a crisis hotline or contact mobile crisis services. The Substance Abuse and Mental Health Services Administration (SAMHSA) funds peer-based recovery programs and statewide consumer networks, and it even declares on its website, "Peer Support Recovery Is the Future of Behavioral Health."

Peer mentoring can boost both physical and mental health – and, in fact, peer programs have integrated "whole health" management.[11] Emory University researchers conducted a randomized study of the Health and Recovery Peer program, a peer-led self-management program for general medical conditions. Four hundred participants who had serious mental illness and at least one chronic medical condition were recruited from community mental health clinics. Patients who received peer mentoring reported greater improvements in both their physical and mental health quality of life. Dr. Wendy Tiegreen, who is now director of Medicaid's Coordination and Health System Innovation at the Department of Behavioral Health & Developmental Disabilities (DBHDD), says, "I have not seen a single thing that has impacted public-sector mental health globally more than peer support ... There's not been a single thing that has changed things more than just that concept of

---

[10] Marill, M. C. (2019). Beyond twelve steps, peer-supported mental health care. *Health Affairs* 38(6): 896–901.

[11] Trust for America's Health (n.d.). Pain in the nation: the drug, alcohol and suicide crises and need for a national resilience strategy. Retrieved from www.tfah.org/report-details/pain-in-the-nation.

recovery and hope."[12] The role of nonclinical peer support is now a core part of the behavioral health workforce nationally, as forty-eight states and the District of Columbia have or are developing a system of certifying peer specialists who can join care teams in varied settings from emergency departments and crisis centers to community programs.[13]

The principles of relational health encourage the development of systems and environments that promote health and health equity. Providers and health care leaders must begin an attitudinal shift that focuses on nonmedical factors and invests in programs that take a holistic view of health.

Obstacles to Change

One of the core difficulties of investing in social networks – pursuing relational health policies to their logical conclusion – is that it requires a focus on the roots of health epidemics, not their manifestations. There will continue to be demands for products and services, many relying on sophisticated technology to address, that react to health problems that are relational at their core. The emergence of robot cats and the explosion of similar technologies, despite their merits, force broader questions concerning the policy values they reflect, questions that heavily impact what lies ahead for the epidemics highlighted in this book. Innovative technological devices (e.g., robots, remote monitoring, or apps to improve all kinds of habits) can be more widely accessible to people than more traditional services provided by strained public health systems.[14] Tailored devices that are designed to address social isolation and other social ills can provide immediate solutions to communities that may be cash-strapped or geographically remote and lack access to in-person care.

Robot devices that simulate emotion can be viewed as one end of a continuum in which the technology is primarily intended to provide companionship – that is, to substitute for human companionship. Other technologies – such as an app that provides feedback to aid habit formation or smart technology that measures and tracks blood glucose levels that health care providers can monitor remotely – do not portend to substitute for human interaction. Some technology, rather than trying to simulate companionship, can even serve to facilitate the development of supportive

[12] Druss, B. G., Singh, M., von Esenwein, S. A., et al. (2018). Peer-led self-management of general medical conditions for patients with serious mental illnesses: a randomized trial. *Psychiatric Services* 69(5): 529–535. https://doi.org/10.1176/appi.ps.201700352

[13] Marill, Beyond twelve steps.   [14] Trust for America's Health, Pain in the nation.

communities. Social networking services that are specifically designed to aid in supporting health habits, such as weight loss or substance use modification, can provide social support through digital communities.[15] These can offer group encouragement, individualized (digital) inter- actions, and the exchange of personal data and recommendations between patients and providers. These devices and services can serve vital functions and reach more people than could otherwise be served by our current health care system.

Along with the potential of such technology, it is essential that the crises upon which this book focuses are also addressed through more compre- hensive priorities and better resource allocation. These technologies can be considered as a way to *augment* – making them better and more accessible – evidence-based reforms to health promotion and how health care is delivered. Otherwise, these devices run the risk of becoming substitutes for these necessary reforms, and the technological equivalent of the med- icalization of social problems – that is, contributing to the problem instead of providing a solution. The possibilities, as well as the limits, of technol- ogy have been starkly evident during the COVID-19 crisis.

We are at a moment of opportunity as our culture confronts the realities of mutual interconnectedness, the costs of its absence, and its centrality for our individual and collective health. This is an apt time to change the cultural narrative in the United States from one that attributes health as coming from individual decisions to one that recognizes that achieving long-term positive health outcomes relies on the relational components of health; that improving neighborhood, community, family, and peer net- works offers the most productive avenues to both address health crises and to improve population health. We must progress actively toward these goals and make use of the current momentum in this direction. Spurred by the Affordable Care Act's emphasis on prevention and an uptick of studies that have demonstrated the potential returns to health care from invest- ments in social services, health policy reformers have a growing interest in the impact of nonmedical determinants of health on both health outcomes and costs.[16]

For relational health to be realized both in the mitigation of health crises and in the daily delivery of care, we must be prepared to reprioritize what

[15] Ashrafian, H., Toma, T., Harling, L., et al. (2014). Social networking strategies that aim to reduce obesity have achieved significant although modest results. *Health Affairs (Project Hope)* 33(9): 1641–1647. https://doi.org/10.1377/hlthaff.2014.0370

[16] Taylor, L. A. (2018). How do we fund flourishing? Maybe not through health care. *Hastings Center Report* 48(S3): S62–S66. https://doi.org/10.1002/hast.916

we consider as worthwhile investments in health. An obstacle to overcome is the lack of widespread recognition that the societal forces that shape our preferences and lifestyles are deeply entrenched. As is the case with obesity (and until recent legal interventions, opioid use disorder), major industries exist that profit from maintaining these behaviors. The rates of obesity are unlikely to change significantly when so much of the country is awash in environments that promote obesity, and where enormous marketing and sales budgets are devoted to targeted advertising to exploit our vulnerabilities and get us hooked on unhealthy products, effectively shaping our preferences starting as toddlers. That the broader unhealthy food environment needs to change is clear, and many prominent food policy experts have articulated excellent proposals for necessary changes. These are politically difficult issues, however, and many are discouragingly slow to implement because of resistance from industry.

Conclusion: Relational Health and More

The extensive upheaval, beginning in 2020, to our typical patterns of daily life has been referred to as a liminal phase, the "time out of time" when society is no longer what it was, but is not yet what it will be. These years are the "betwixt and between" where the rules were broken and we are provided a chance to reassess what we really need. In a public interview, Dr. Sherry Turkle expressed a positive outlook on the potential social upheaval that COVID can bring, both regarding our relationship with technology and more generally how our society is operating: "We've had a chance [through the COVID pandemic] to step away from our country and see it at a distance in so many areas of life . . . and seeing things fresh and seeing them anew gives us a chance to come back and act more deliberately in all of these areas."[17]

This is true not just for our health policy but also for the way we perceive ourselves in our modern society. If we can develop a stronger appreciation for how our decisions and behaviors are influenced by social factors at the level of communities, families, and peers, then we can better recognize the impact of investing in these social structures. This may come in part from demanding different kinds of messaging and education of our youth. Our cultural narratives – that we are immersed in at very young ages – of strong

---

[17] WBUR (2021). Sherry Turkle on what a year of COVID teaches us about empathy. Retrieved from: www.wbur.org/onpoint/2021/03/11/web-extra-sherry-turkle-on-what-a-year-of-covid-teaches-us-about-empathy.

willpower being the answer to our individual and societal struggles and approaching challenges with a "go it alone" approach will not help us to tackle our modern health crises. Instead, more than ever, the value of how our social networks can contribute to solving these health crises needs to be fully realized.

Index

Page numbers in *italic* refer to figures

Printed by Printforce, United Kingdom